Salomon Brothers
1910-1985

Salomon Brothers
1910-1985

ADVANCING
TO
LEADERSHIP

by
Robert Sobel

Photo Credits

p. 12, Culver Pictures; p. 42, Jack Manning/NYT Pictures;
p. 99, The New York Times; p. 114, Ken Regan/Camera 5;
pp. 116 & 117, Simon Nathan/Time Magazine;
p. 135, David Stoecklein/Photo Unique.

Text Acknowledgments

p. 49, excerpt from article on Swift & Co. bond issue.
Copyright ©1935 by The New York Times Company.
Reprinted by Permission. p. 99, excerpt from article
on Benjamin Levy. Copyright ©1966 by The New York
Times Company. Reprinted by Permission.

Table of Contents

Introduction

The investment banking firm of Salomon Brothers Inc has prospered greatly since its modest beginnings in 1910. That January a group of four people, the three brothers — Arthur, Herbert, and Percy — along with a clerk, Ben Levy, formed a money brokerage with only $5,000 in capital. By its 75th year, the firm had become one of the world's leading underwriters of capital issues and an innovative force in the financial marketplace. That small office at 80 Broadway had grown to an organization of 3,500 in 10 offices on four continents. Salomon Brothers had become one of the great powers in global finance.

That story of expansion and diversification is a remarkable one, and it occupies an important place in the economic story of 20th century America. It is a history of great individual enterprise, entrepreneurial skill, teamwork and willingness to take risks, bolstered by tireless research to improve decision-making and the effective conduct of business.

Accompanying these vital elements has been a long-term principle of taking positive actions and positions that benefit corporate clients and the general economy. The decisions made by Salomon Brothers have always sought to yield profits both for the firm and for the members of the business community with whom it deals. The range and extent of the relationships that have been formed are impressively broad: small companies, large corporations, state and local governments, agencies, and sovereign nations.

Throughout these 75 years of intense activity countless commitments have been made, decisions have been taken, great successes have been achieved and, of course, failures and missteps have been recorded. What is unique about Salomon Brothers is that despite the fundamental expansion in range and type of undertakings, a thread of continuity was created from the outset. The firm has forged a singular character in the way that it goes about its business and in the way it deals with its own people and with its customers.

This history of Salomon Brothers recounts the factual events of the firm's dramatic rise to worldwide influence. More important, it dwells on the interplay of people and generations who have achieved those successes. It emphasizes the relevance of attitudes and intentions that have stretched from the very first days to the present, and the attention that is being paid to maintaining these essential principles in the volatile and demanding future.

In the early years, Salomon Brothers & Hutzler was a small factor in the highly specialized business of money brokerage. It competed against many others who had more capital and personnel in an environment very different from today. Occupying the pinnacle on Wall Street in the 1910s and 1920s were a handful of large financial institutions. J.P. Morgan & Co., First National, National City, and Guaranty Trust were directed by an elite. This group worked with a German Jewish group of financiers, headed by Jacob Schiff of Kuhn, Loeb, whose roots were in the brawling 19th century industrial expansion.

Arthur, Herbert, and Percy Salomon survived in this world of intense competition. One of the most important reasons was Arthur's insistence that the firm's pledge always be honored at all costs. By the 1920s Salomon was known as one of the more trustworthy firms in that period before establishment of the Securities and Exchange Commission. This was Arthur Salomon's most important legacy.

With integrity and a respect for its importance, Arthur Salomon made it possible to give creative vent to ambitions and expansion. The firm was an opportunist in the best sense of the term and constantly sought innovative new areas for its energies. The reason that the brothers united with Morton Hutzler in 1910 was to obtain access to his New York Stock Exchange seat. In 1914, the house was one of the first to recognize the promise offered by the new Federal Reserve System and quickly registered to become an active participant. Thus it shared in the government securities market during its expansion in World War I, and was an increasingly significant factor in bonds during the Great Bull Market of the 1920s.

When most investment houses joined in the "capital strike" following passage of the Securities Exchange Act of 1934, Salomon Brothers & Hutzler responded by serving as agent for a bond offering for Swift & Co., breaking the logjam that had developed in the capital markets. In later years, Salomon Brothers led the way in developing zero coupon bonds and creating novel methods whereby businesses could obtain needed capital and help institutional investors find new instruments for their investments. Its decisions were crucial in creating mortgage-backed securities, which have become one of the largest and most important financial activities in the industry.

Risks always have been taken, in those early years as well as now. By acting as it did in the Swift offering, for example, Salomon Brothers incurred the displeasure of Wall Street's Establishment. But the American financial system was changing rapidly, and as the Old Guard attempted to maintain the *status quo*, Salomon Brothers and others moved to meet the new challenges. In later years one of the most dramatic examples of this was the creation in the early 1960s of what came to be known as "The Fearsome Foursome," comprised of Salomon Brothers, Blyth, Merrill Lynch, and Lehman, a group which united to compete against the Old Guard in bidding for corporate underwritings. This was followed by "Guerrilla Groups," which under Salomon's leadership did the same for municipal bonds.

Another principle originated when Arthur Salomon insisted that the firm stand prepared to repurchase whatever it sold. This was to accommodate clients. His successors carried on in this tradition, and earned a reputation for making efficient markets and having great distribution and placement powers. It was as important during the dog days of the 1930s, when markets barely moved, as in the hectic years of the 1960s, 1970s and 1980s, when placement and the willingness to take large positions became prized qualities. Salomon became a major player in the block market, buying and selling large amounts of stock from clients at a time when other firms shrank from it.

By then, too, Salomon Brothers was starting to reap the potential planted by Arthur Salomon in the early years and nourished by his successors. The firm grew in prestige due to the size and scope of its operations. Barely noticed on the Street in the 1950s, Salomon was truly instrumental in helping save New York City from bankruptcy two decades later. The firm that had difficulty in convincing large corporations to accept its services in the early years was later a key factor in the decisions that saved Chrysler and GEICO.

All this manifests a high degree of flexibility. At Salomon Brothers, academic concepts such as management by objective, tables of organization, and many others taught in the business schools are not always easy to apply in understanding the operations of the firm. Salomon is not and never was a highly structured organization in the conduct of its main business — research, market making and investment banking. Arthur Salomon insisted that his salesmen and traders combine their efforts, and to assure this Salomon Brothers did not pay individual commissions then, and does not do so today.

The purpose is to create greater teamwork than is encountered elsewhere in the industry and a greater flexibility of structure, more in the mold of a medieval guild than a contemporary investment bank. At Salomon, newcomers begin as apprentices, working with a trader or salesman, and after a while they start trading or selling on a modest level, always observed by the veteran. In time they become journeymen and eventually masters. Throughout, they work closely with their peers and seniors, and eventually become mentors to the next group of newcomers.

This tradition was created in the early days and honed by the first generation, young men who arrived at the firm in the 1910s and 1920s. They fashioned the ethic that survived through the Great Depression, World War II and the slow bond market that followed.

The originators, under the guidance of Arthur Salomon's leadership, passed it on to the second generation.

Led by the strong and imaginative direction of Arthur's nephew, Bill Salomon, these men joined the firm in the 1950s. This group included John Gutfreund, who furthered the culture and refined it, and under whose leadership Salomon Brothers has arrived in the first rank of investment banking. These individuals, who now direct the firm's destiny, are aware of its heritage, and they know that one of their major tasks is to inspire newly arrived young people with the same spirit.

At first blush it may seem the self-educated traders and salesmen who worked beside the founders had little in common with the bright, highly educated, energetic young people who now populate the firm. There is also a marked difference between the new people of the 1950s and those of the 1980s; John Gutfreund noted that "in the current world, I would not be high on the roster for hire" at today's Salomon Brothers. But look again, and you'll see evidence of that aforementioned core. For example, Arthur Salomon wrote in 1914:

> I always liked this business and I do not believe a man can succeed unless he loves his work. However, I am not prepared to give you any formula for success in Wall Street as I believe every man must work out his own course. Of this I am certain — that no man can succeed who is not a worker and who does not value his integrity above all things.

In 1984, John Gutfreund told a group of entering trainees:

> Discipline and integrity are vital. There isn't anything like a half-truth; either it's so or it isn't. Everything in our business is still an oral confirmation. And the written confirmation which comes later is almost like an afterthought. Everything you say or do commits this firm. The main part of our discipline is truth. You'll be much more truthful here than in the rest of your life where you might have to tell white lies to get along.

The importance of positive change from generation to generation was early realized by those who participated in creating and carrying on that heritage. One of them was Jonas Ottens, who joined Salomon Brothers in 1918 and is often singled out by many of the firm's present leaders as one who delighted in taking newcomers under his wing and instructing them in trading and sales, capital retention and, most important, the Salomon Brothers way of operating.

James Massey is a managing director and Executive Committee member who has responsibility for recruitment and training, as well as sales. He believes that the person who will prove most valuable is the one who "can clone himself, multiply — if one person who runs a sales unit can train ten others to do the same thing he does, he's much more valuable to us than one individual who is a superstar who can't train anyone. Salomon has gotten to where it is through the efforts of people who have leveraged their own talents and experience." Thus Salomon's veterans make certain that their experience, knowledge, and ethic are passed on to those who follow and in time will succeed them.

At Salomon Brothers today, John Gutfreund is usually found at his desk right on the main trading floor, continually prepared to consult with traders and salesmen, both veterans and newcomers. In this he follows in the footsteps of Bill Salomon. And the same accessibility is true for others in top management. This egalitarian organization may confuse bystanders who aren't aware of the firm's tradition and how it developed; it can appear to be somewhat disorganized. Yet this attitude toward cooperation has provided Salomon with the adaptability that served it well during the markets of pre-World War I America, just as it does for the more complex challenges of the world today.

Markets today are more hectic and mercurial than at any time in modern history. Hundreds of billions of dollars can wash from the eastern and western shores of the Atlantic and Pacific at the slightest change of an interest rate or a blip in some arcane statistic. Large institutions place tens of millions of dollars a day into securities, prepared to switch or swap them, and to move at a moment's notice.

Major corporations restructure their debt and equity situations so as to momentarily profit from changes in market conditions and government regulations. Money managers move in and out of dollars, yen, deutschemarks, pounds, and other currencies, all the while keeping an eye on political and financial capitals in attempts to assess possibilities. Thus, Salomon Brothers must be prepared to meet the needs of clients by utilizing old concepts in an efficient way and developing new ones when called for.

This is the era of the triangular financial universe, where round-the-clock activities are conducted in step with the sun as it moves over New York, on to Tokyo, then to London, and back to New York. At any given time Salomon Brothers has a portfolio in excess of $11 billion on a net basis, which is shifted along with the sun.

As Salomon's New York office closes, its Tokyo operation awakens. It has one of the largest non-Japanese financial presences in that country, and its relationship with the Japanese is hardly new. In 1910, Percy Salomon was selling American bonds to Japanese banks and insurance firms wishing to diversify away from their home islands because of fear of an earthquake.

When Tokyo's day is done, activity shifts to London, where Salomon Brothers is the second largest underwriter and one of the fastest-moving firms in the city.

But all are part of the whole. The young trader you might have seen in London last week might be encountered in Stockholm the next; the managing director in Tokyo will be in New York for consultation several times a year. The Salomon spirit, nurtured in small money-changing operations in those halcyon pre-World War I years, is now visible on an international scale.

Chapter I

A Modest Launching
1910-1914

Salomon Brothers opened for business in a modest office near Wall Street on the first Monday in 1910. New Year's Day dawned that year on a confident and optimistic New York that was preparing itself for the inauguration of Mayor-elect William S. Gaynor. Changes were taking place in everyday life in the growing city and there was a palpable quickening in the pace of activities. The subways were being constructed, and both inhabitants and tourists wondered at the 45-story Singer Building which had been completed in 1908. It was a harbinger of many other "skyscrapers" to come. Electrification was rapidly expanding, and this was altering the fabric of life for middle class New Yorkers.

Along 14th Street and on Broadway, motion picture theaters were replacing the old nickelodeons. By 1910 there were almost 9,000 such theaters across the nation, and a new industry clearly was arriving. Courtland Field Bishop, President of the Aero Club of America, spoke glowingly of the future of the airplane, while young David Sarnoff was preparing his ideas for the creation of "the radio music box." On that same New Year's Day a notice appeared in the city's press that was a vivid sign of the times. The New York Horse Exchange between 50th and 51st Streets was going to be razed to make way for a theater. The day of the buggy clearly was drawing to a close and would soon be replaced by that of the automobile.

An era truly was ending. Transformations in travel and in energy were among the most noticeable, but most important for the Salomons and other brokers of the decade was the decline of fixed, immutable capital markets. A new era of dynamism and uncertainty had arrived, even though few were able to realize it at the time. In the summer of 1910 Americans gazed with wonder at Halley's comet, supposedly an omen of novel things to come. So they did — but not in the ways most expected.[1]

This was the environment in which the three sons of Ferdinand Salomon established their business. Ferdinand was a money broker, the same as his father. This meant he arranged short term loans for securities brokers and others at banks and trust companies. It is probable that the Salomons had been engaged in this business in Alsace-Lorraine, their home province on the Franco-German border. Ferdinand emigrated to the United States as a young boy and became a part of the hard-working 19th century Jewish community of New York City. He married Sophia Heilbron, a strong-willed Englishwoman who was a fine pianist and temperamentally quite different from her stolid, religious husband. In fact, she never did take out citizenship papers, and for all of her life considered herself British.

Despite that ambivalence about life in America, Sophia made a home for her family in a brownstone at Madison Avenue near 132nd Street. There she gave birth to four sons: Arthur (more commonly known as A.K.) in 1880, Leo in 1881, Percy in the next year, and Herbert in 1884. By the turn of the century all but Leo, who had become an insurance broker, were working for their father in his office in the financial district, where he conducted a small money brokerage business.[2]

In 1907 the nation suffered through one of its periodic financial crises, when the collapse of the Knickerbocker Trust caused a run on the banks. Had it not been for J.P. Morgan's intercession, the entire national banking edifice might have collapsed. As it was, dozens of brokerages and money dealers were driven out of business. The Salomons managed to survive, and in the buoyant aftermath of the panic their future seemed reasonably bright. Whether their business would have developed beyond money brokerage is uncertain, however. Ferdinand Salomon had done nothing else for three decades and had never shown any inclination to change or expand. But a domestic crisis was brewing.

Ferdinand was orthodox in his religious views and refused to do business on Saturdays, the Jewish sabbath, in a time when Wall Street was open for half of the day. The sons believed that one of the reasons the firm was not growing as rapidly as it could was its refusal to meet clients' needs on Saturday. While Ferdinand was in synagogue the sons would go to the district and transact business. It was the classic American confrontation of generations, common in immigrant groups of that period and even later. In the case of the Salomon family, this difference in attitude and practice finally broke the relationship.[3]

During the period of this father-and-sons conflict, Ferdinand's marriage was also breaking up. Early in 1909 he moved from the house on Madison Avenue and obtained a divorce. On June 9, 1909, Ferdinand took out citizenship papers, and soon after remarried. The sons sided with their mother, and shortly after the divorce they decided to break away from their father and start their own business.

When it became clear that Ferdinand intended to retire, his clerk, the reticent but loyal Benjamin Levy, opted to join the sons. The brothers raised $5,000 from their own savings and a small loan from Percy's in-laws. On Monday, January 3, 1910, they opened shop in a tiny office at 80 Broadway, calling their newly created group "Salomon Brothers." This event was not noted in the general or financial press. In reality the Salomons remained all but anonymous — except to their clients and competitors — for most of the next decade.[4]

The financial district at the time of the birth of Salomon Brothers was strikingly different from what it is today, both in appearance and functions. The seven-year-old New York Stock Exchange Building was in place at the junction of Wall and Broad Streets, across the way from J.P. Morgan & Co. On the north side of Wall Street was the Subtreasury, erected on the site of Federal Hall, where George Washington had been inaugurated President in 1789.

Along Broad Street, near Exchange Place, was the open-door Curb Market, where brokers transacted business and sent messages to clerks hanging out of windows at the Mills Building. Down the street, at Broad and Beaver, was

Arthur, Herbert and Percy Salomon (left to right) founded a money brokerage firm in 1910 and soon were joined by New York Stock Exchange member Morton Hutzler. The firm then expanded into trading corporate and municipal issues.

the NYSE's rival, the Consolidated Stock Exchange, while in between them, office buildings housed the headquarters of many of the nation's biggest corporations.

The financial institutions, which have always been the true heart of the district, had offices on Wall Street or in a block demarcated by Broadway, Nassau, Cedar and Liberty Streets. There were more than 100 banks and 35 trust companies in that area, and some 23 banks and seven trusts had offices on Wall Street. These institutions were domiciled in buildings that either bore their names or were owned by them. In less prominent places, often in cubbyhole offices, were the smaller investment banks, virtually all of which have disappeared or been merged out of existence.

In 1910 as today, information was the lifeblood of the market, and throughout the business day tickers, telephones and hundreds of messengers connected the firms in a complex network, providing the veins and arteries through which flowed money and credit. Middlemen such as the Salomon brothers lubricated the mechanism by gathering and passing on information to bring parties together.

There was a tendency for outsiders to judge the health of the district by activities at the NYSE, which was in the doldrums following the strong recovery after the 1907 Panic.[5] Then, as now, equities were only a part of the Wall Street scene, and at that time they were not a very important one. New bond listings at the NYSE invariably surpassed those of stocks. In 1910 the Exchange accepted for trading $297 million in equities, but $571 million in bonds. Since bonds were continually being called or maturing, the totals for debt and equities were closer. Still, there were $11.7 billion in stocks in this period against $12.7 billion in bonds at the NYSE.

Industrial bonds were far more important than governments, and more than half of the former were accounted for by the railroads. The manufacturing offerings trailed, followed by those of utilities. Foreign governments had close to $2 billion in bonds outstanding, against less than $900 million in United States obligations and $449 million in New York City securities.[6]

The reasons for the small amount of federal paper outstanding and traded will become clear when it is understood that federal expenditures for 1910 came to $694 million. There was a deficit of $19 million, which *The New York Times* called "scandalous." President William Howard Taft explained that this was due to the lingering effects of the 1907 Panic, and promised it would be eliminated the following year, which it was — the surplus came to $11 million — due to spending cuts and an increase in tariff collections.

Given this kind of situation one can easily understand why industrials dominated the bond list, and federal paper was relatively unimportant. For that matter, so were state and local bonds, some $4 billion of which in that year were outstanding. There was no distinction between tax exempts and corporates, for the simple reason that interest payments were not taxed as income.

The NYSE listings were a fraction of the total paper outstanding. Not included were those stocks in young and untested firms traded at the Curb and Consolidated, and debt obligations of domestic firms which for reasons of size and quality didn't seek listing, as well as inactive issues for which brokers and dealers provided auctions not unlike those which had existed in the early 19th century.

The financial institutions monitored these markets carefully, as did the over 60 life insurance and 260 fire and marine insurance firms whose offices were in the district. American industry demanded capital in order to expand, governments needed funds to operate, and the banks, trusts, and insurance firms were constantly seeking investment opportunities and outlets for their surplus cash.

This is a bare outline of the community in which individual brokers such as the Salomons operated. The brothers were in competition with other small money brokers and the NYSE's money desk, and had to scramble to obtain business. Each morning the Salomons would travel from bank to bank to speak with the managers, discovering which of them had surpluses to lend on that day.

Arthur was in command of the firm and was its chief strategist, and he dealt with the major institutions: Morgan, National Bank of Commerce, Chase, and the other large ones. Herbert went to the secondary institutions while Percy, more retiring than the others, covered foreign banks, the Japanese in particular.[7] They also went to brokerage firms to find out their requirements. Ben Levy remained in the office, manning the telephone and taking orders to buy and sell, which he transmitted to Arthur, Percy, and Herbert when they returned from their rounds.

The Salomons started out as classic middlemen. They would arrange the loans from the banks at 30, 60, or 90 days, occasionally longer. Then they placed these loans with the brokers who were seeking call money and had to put up collateral, usually in the form of securities. The net cost to both sides would be slightly lower than was available at the money desk. "We would arrange the loans," recalled Ben Levy 67 years later, "But the brothers wouldn't take positions in money or deal in what today are known as money futures." This was a risky area, for just as long term rates were firm, the shorts were highly volatile. In January, 1910, call money

Page from a 1912 ledger lists loans arranged by Salomon Brothers. As a newcomer in the investment community, the firm quickly established its reputation for rapid and superior service among institutional portfolio managers and major banks.

in New York averaged 4.7 percent, went to 2.8 percent in February, and by May was back to 3.6 percent.[8]

Most of the loans arranged by the Salomons were for 90 days, on which the brothers received a commission of 1/32nd of 1 percent, so that in the case of a $100,000 loan the charge would come to $31.25. For a 30-day loan the Salomons received a third of that figure, or $10.41, while a "double commission" of 1/8th of 1 percent came with a half-year loan.

In early January, 1910, the firm arranged for a loan of $100,000 for four months at 4.5 percent interest from the National Bank of Commerce to a NYSE member, entered in the books as "F. (St.) Goar." During the first month of operations the Salomons arranged 41 loans totaling $7,025,000, on which the gross commissions came to $2,823.58.[9]

The Salomons were marginal factors in a marginal segment of the industry. In order simply to survive they had to provide rapid and superior service, and to obtain a reputation for honesty and integrity, since price cutting on so low a margin was impossible. They succeeded to the point where Salomon Brothers had become a major force in their limited field within a few months.

It appears the Salomons — led by Arthur — soon decided to seek other, related outlets for their talents and resources. Their physical assets were no more than the one-room, partitioned office, three desks, and Benjamin Levy's telephone. Working from that level, they amassed experience as middlemen in the district and became fairly well-known and respected. Most important, they proved then and later to have a keen understanding of the fluctuations in the money and bond markets.

The Salomons opted to experiment, knowing they had little to lose, and entered the bond market, which, as noted above, was quite different from what it is today. During this period, financial institutions and trust funds were limited by law as to the kinds of securities to be maintained in their reserve funds. In most jurisdictions, common and even preferred stocks didn't qualify, and so the demand for bonds was much stronger than it would be later on. Then, too, stock ownership was far less widespread. Individuals who purchased shares in any but the bluest of blue chips — the large railroads, for example — did so as either speculators or manipulators. Prudent people owned bonds; gamblers "took flyers" in stocks.

The Salomons weren't interested in these individual investors, however; they dealt with the insurance companies, banks and trust companies that were their clients. They set out to thoroughly learn their needs and meet them.

Thus, Arthur, Percy, or Herbert might discover that one of their trust clients was seeking a certain quality 30-year railroad bond yielding 4 percent. They would have also learned that another client had paper of that description and wished to dispose of it. The Salomons would then purchase the bonds in the morning and deliver them in the afternoon. In this fashion they did not place any of their firm's capital at risk, and they profited from the spread between the buy and sell prices.

It is clear this was done on a small scale. In those days it was customary for brokers and others offering bonds for sale to advertise in the financial press and business pages. Significantly, the Salomons did not feel the need to place such notices for the first decade of their existence as a firm.

In both money and bond operations, the Salomons competed not only with outside dealers but also with NYSE members operating from the floor. It had been evident from the outset that their business would benefit from having access to the Exchange, but purchasing a seat was well beyond their means. In 1910, the price of one averaged $79,000, which was about twice the amount of money the company earned in that year. The only alternatives were to remain on the outside or to unite with a cooperating member. The Salomons chose the latter course, and that spring joined with Morton Hutzler, who had a seat. Under the terms of an agreement signed on April 16, they formed a partnership, which initially would run for one year, with each partner putting up $1,250 and all sharing equally in the profits. The new entity, Salomon Brothers & Hutzler, opened for business on May 2, 1910.

The scion of an old Baltimore family that owned the city's largest department store, Hutzler had worked there for a while and found merchandising not to his liking. In 1905, at the age of 26, he relocated to New York, purchased a seat on the NYSE for $81,000, and operated as a "two-dollar broker," which meant he stood ready to execute orders for both Exchange members and non-members for that amount of money. Hutzler had an edge in that his brother-in-law, Clarence Hausman, was a principal at A.A. Hausman & Co., one of the largest multiple-office brokerage houses of the time. Presumably Hutzler obtained some of his business through this relationship. Indeed, this connection may have determined his decision to make the original move to New York.[10]

Some two-dollar brokers were both famous and wealthy. Hutzler was not one of them, and this may have been the reason he was receptive to the idea of coming in with the Salomons. Thereafter he could execute floor orders for Salomon clients, while the brothers could expand their influence through Hutzler's somewhat limited but still important contacts. Nonetheless, the fact is that Hutzler's impact upon the company never extended beyond the bounds of the NYSE. Even there he had to be assisted by clerks and, later on, by other partners. He frequently remained on the sidelines during quiet sessions, while Salomon employees handled most of the actual work. Still, his seat was useful, for through it the Salomons were able to trade listed bonds for their clients, and so entered that field in a small way.[11]

Salomon Brothers & Hutzler expanded their business and entered into the bankers acceptance field. This was, and still is, a familiar form of commercial paper, being simply an agreement on the part of a bank to pay specific bills for one of its customers when they came due. Merchandisers often paid for supplies with bankers acceptances, which meant the receiver had to hold on to it for weeks or even months before it could be presented to the bank for payment. Secure enough (they were guaranteed by the bank), acceptances still required the holder to forgo use of the money during this period.

Moreover, there was an interest rate risk involved. For example, at the time of the origination of a six-month acceptance the going interest rate might have been 4 percent. Suppose it rose to 6 percent shortly thereafter; the holder would then have paper that was less valuable, since his forgone interest was not 50 percent higher. In 1911, the rate fluctuated from 3.6 percent to 4.6 percent.[12]

In order to avoid this and to eliminate whatever risk existed, the holder might sell his acceptances to a dealer in such paper at a discount from the face value. This was an important activity in the city, and it would appear the Salomons did a lively business in the paper. They flourished to the point where it made sense to advertise by way of a name change; they now titled themselves "The Discount House of Salomon Brothers & Hutzler."

Other diversifications followed: rail equipment trust certificates, tax anticipation notes, federal land bank notes, foreign currency, and gold certificates. Almost any form of paper for which Salomon Brothers & Hutzler could act as an intermediary and receive a commission, or in the case of commercial paper, hold for short periods before redemption, was taken on. To develop the latter business the firm required short term capital, which meant that it too had to enter into borrowings to expand its bond dealings.

The brothers realized there was only so much that might be accomplished by acting solely as middlemen. It made more sense to accumulate an inventory of bonds and then go out and try to sell them. For example, many individuals purchased bonds one or two at a time, while trust companies preferred to buy them in round lots. The odd lots were difficult to sell, and so often had to be disposed of at a lower price than ordinarily would have been received. The Salomons and others in the business would purchase such paper, seek out others of the same issue (also at a lower price) and then put them together in a round lot to offer a trust company. While waiting they would receive interest, and if successful, a profit on the sale as well.

Another of their activities was to purchase new issues that were unpopular due to the size of the underwriting, and then await the proper purchaser. In this period it wasn't unusual for a rural county to float a $20,000 bond issue at, say, 4½ percent, maturing serially from the date of issue at $2,000 each year. There wasn't much of a market for such bonds, and so they had to pay slightly higher rates. The

Salomons might take them up, in anticipation that shortly one or another of their clients would like to have just such paper in his portfolio. In this almost serendipitous fashion the firm was inching its way into becoming an underwriter as well as a dealer.[13]

Such a departure by the Salomons required taking more risks. By then they had become expert at acting as conduits through which capital flowed. In order to enter the bond field directly, the firm would also be required to perform as vessels in which the capital would be held. The original in-and-out business had not required them to acquire any

Salomon Brothers' first office was situated just off Wall Street, the core of New York's financial district.

particularly strong expertise in bond values, or to make projections on yields or judgments on quality. Furthermore, there had been no need to develop trading techniques.

Now Hutzler could remain at the Exchange executing orders, but the brothers would have to devote less time to canvassing the banks and trust companies and more to studying bonds. Moreover, additional personnel, preferably experienced in this area, would have to be hired or taken in as partners. The new people would have to bring in substantial new capital as well as contacts.

One of the first of these partners was Charles Bernheim, who came into the firm in 1913. He was wealthy in his own right as a successful shirt manufacturer, and he was related to Jerome Hanauer, who was a general partner at Kuhn, Loeb. Bernheim became active at the bond desk and helped develop this end of the business, while the brothers swiftly developed a sophisticated understanding of the many nuances of this complex financial activity.[14]

In the last year of peace before the outbreak of World War I, The Discount House of Salomon Brothers & Hutzler not only had become generally established, but had created an atmosphere conducive to future growth. The base of action as an intermediary was firmly in place, and a strong initiative in bond trading and marketing had been taken. Yet there had to be limits to the firm's ambitions. Salomon Brothers & Hutzler dealt with banks, trusts and insurance companies. Arthur understood that important corporations and prominent individuals transacted business with the district's prestigious traditional firms and did not even consider employing Salomon or other firms with the same special outlook, background and circumstances.

In 1914 the Salomons' achievements rested in maintaining the good will and respect of institutional portfolio managers. The firm also served the major investment banks in any way that was required, hoping that by so doing it eventually might obtain some crumbs from the underwriting table. This was not a forbidding prospect for a firm that had begun so precariously only four years earlier, and yet it hardly seemed to hold out prospects for future greatness.

Chapter II

Into the Mainstream
1915-1928

A congressional committee conducted hearings on banking reform in the early years of Woodrow Wilson's first term as president. Throughout them its counsel, Samuel Untermyer, castigated the "Money Trust." During the course of the investigations, Untermyer and J.P. Morgan held the following dialogue:

> *Untermyer*: Is not commercial credit based primarily upon money or property?
>
> *Morgan*: No, sir: the first thing is character.
>
> *Untermyer*: Before money or property?
>
> *Morgan*: Before money or anything else. Money cannot buy it.[1]

It became perfectly clear in the testimony that Untermyer did not believe Morgan, and that the banker wondered how anyone claiming to understand the workings of American finance could doubt the accuracy of his statement. In this atmosphere of friction between business and the reform element, Salomon Brothers & Hutzler was expanding its operations.

The firm was establishing a good reputation and proving its eagerness to serve clients. But in the early years its scope of activity was limited and its capital resources were meager. In the world of American finance of the period, this would have managed to provide the brothers and their partner with a comfortable but hardly affluent existence. However, the financial markets underwent significant change in the next few years. The European war forever altered world history, and the international importance of America was immensely increased. Both developments favorably influenced the course of the Salomons' business.

Reform Democrats captured control of both the White House and Congress in 1913, and one of their goals was a thoroughgoing overhaul of the banking system. On June 23, President Woodrow Wilson declared the need for new legislation "...so that the banks [would] be the instruments, not the masters, of business and of individual enterprise." Out of this came the Glass-Owen Act, which was passed by Congress on December 23, 1913, and signed into law. A new central bank, the Federal Reserve System, was established under the terms of the legislation.

The new system's first test came only months later, when the Fed had barely been established. Panics erupted in most of the world's financial markets in late July, 1914, as the great European powers traded ultimatums. The Treasury started pumping funds into the system. But the fears continued, and dire forecasts of impending financial disaster were rampant. But no collapse occurred; quite to the contrary, an economic expansion of unparalleled scope was set off. The United States had been the world's leading debtor nation in 1914, but became its leading creditor only four years later. In this rapid process Wall Street replaced London's Lombard Street as the premier capital center of the world. After a sharp but brief post-war depression, there began a period of even more substantial economic growth for the United States.

Both war and boom had to be financed. In early 1915, the French government received permission to float a $50 million loan in the United States, and in September of the same year another $500 million was loaned to an Anglo-French consortium. By the time the United States entered the conflict in 1917, New York's bankers had loaned the Allies $2.3 billion. When America became a belligerent, the Treasury borrowed heavily to finance America's first major armament program since the Civil War. These lendings accelerated as the American military forces were radically increased. The national debt, which had been only $1.2 billion in 1914, reached $25.5 billion at the end of 1919. This money, too, was raised in the financial district.[2]

Foreign Loans Marketed in the United States, 1914-1917

COUNTRY	AMOUNT (in millions of dollars)
United Kingdom	1250
France	640
Russia	107
Japan	102
Italy	25
Central Powers	35
Others	838

Source: William Shultz and M.R. Caine, *Financial Development of the United States* (New York: Prentice-Hall, 1937), pp. 505-6.

Wall Street experienced prosperity and a level of activity far greater than ever before. The Dow Jones industrial average went from 74.56 on December 12, 1914, to break the 100 level on September 1, 1915, while volume, especially in the bond sector, soared.

Volume of Sales on the NYSE, 1914-1918

YEAR	STOCK SALES (in millions of shares)	BOND SALES (in millions of dollars)			
		Total	Corporate	Government	Foreign, States, Municipal
1914	48	462	427	1	34
1915	173	961	907	3	51
1916	233	1150	845	1	304
1917	186	1057	473	286	300
1918	144	2063	356	1436	271

Source: U.S. Bureau of the Census, *Historical Statistics of the United States, Colonial Times to 1970* (Washington, D.C.: USGPO, 1975), p. 1007.

This situation offered a tremendous opportunity for a firm like Salomon Brothers & Hutzler, which soon outgrew its offices at 80 Broadway. In 1915 the brothers moved to larger but somewhat shabby quarters at 27 Pine Street, not far from the Subtreasury and less than a hundred yards from both the NYSE and J.P. Morgan.[3]

Arthur was prepared temperamentally and financially to enter the underwriting area. However, he lacked the proper social credentials. This was at a time when the old aristocracy still dominated the district. The leading houses — J.P. Morgan; Kuhn, Loeb; Ladenburg Thalmann; Lehman Brothers; Lee, Higginson; N.W. Halsey; and William A. Read — were old-line Protestant or German Jewish firms, and they cooperated with one another much of the time. They were understood to have had a tacit understanding to keep others out of the field. The Salomons lacked the backgrounds of most of their rivals. They had not even attended college and their lineage was unlikely to impress the financial district's elite. Consequently, they were ignored when it came to putting together the syndicates necessary to market industrial securities on a vast scale.

However, Arthur realized that he could do well in government bonds, since these required no such personal or social contacts. Allocations for bonds were made by open bidding, and all could compete in terms of price and size of offering. Salomon Brothers & Hutzler seized the opportunity and soon became a small but respected force in this market. In 1915 the firm participated in the underwriting of a $15 million offering of Argentinian short term notes. Then the house expanded into underwritings of foreign bonds, and became an active participant in this area of the bond market.[4]

The turning point for the Salomons — and other houses outside of the Establishment — came with the passage of the initial Liberty Loan Act in 1917. This authorized the Treasury to borrow up to $5 billion in long term loans at 3½ percent and also to sell $2 billion of short term certificates of indebtedness in anticipation of loan receipts. The first offering, in May, was of $2 billion in bonds, and others followed. By the end of the war more than $17 billion of the paper had been sold, and in 1919 an additional $4.5 billion Victory Loan was floated.[5]

Salomon Brothers & Hutzler registered with the Treasury and became an authorized dealer in United States government securities. (C.F. Childs registered several days earlier. After Childs' demise Salomon became the nation's oldest government paper dealer.) The firm bid on offerings, took delivery of them, and then resold them to their institutional clients. Then Salomon maintained a secondary market in the paper, prepared to offer quotes to customers who might later want to dispose of their holdings. The money brokerage continued, but accounted for a smaller part of the business, and became almost incidental after Arthur developed the government bond sector. Thus, the firm had been substantially transformed by the World War.

Arthur came to develop a view of the post-war markets and a concept of the role Salomon Brothers & Hutzler might play in them that was both realistic and ambitious. The firm remained devoted to making primary and secondary markets in foreign debts, and became known as a specialist in such paper. Its advertisements in the financial pages indicated the Salomons dealt not only in the debt of most European and many Latin American countries and Canada, but municipalities and provinces as well. In addition, the firm both sold and traded in short term U.S. government notes, and constantly sought additional opportunities emerging from the new post-war world order. This persistent quest for new possibilities and markets, which began under Arthur's leadership, continues today and surely is one of the essential hallmarks of the firm.

During the war the Salomons had discounted drafts drawn on European banks. This practice was broadened in 1921 when the Federal Reserve ruled that it would permit American banks to discount six-month import and export paper. (The previous limit had been three months.) An American exporter could now enter an agreement to sell goods to an importer with payment to be made in up to six months. This obligation might be sold at a discount to dealers, in much the same way domestic paper had been sold for decades.

However, there was an important difference; instead of either holding the paper until maturity or placing it with a client, the dealer might sell to the Fed. In the spring of 1921 the Fed reduced the discount rate from 7 percent to 6½ percent, and indicated that future declines were on the way. The option to sell discount paper to the Fed created a situation in which far greater liquidity and marketability could be realized.

Arthur immediately appreciated the implications of this change and stated his position in a newspaper article in early 1922. Instead of marketing international commercial paper on an individual basis as before, the firm could now trade the instruments in somewhat the same fashion as stocks and bonds.[6]

In the spring of 1921, Arthur had announced in another of his articles that Salomon would start dealing in international commercial paper. It was expected that the firm's discount would be around one-eighth of one percent a month. This meant that if the current short term money rates were 6½ percent, the Salomons would discount the paper at 6⅝ percent. He further suggested that a market be created for such vehicles to utilize practices common at London's commodity markets, the grain and cotton markets in the United States, and stock options pioneered on Wall Street in the late 19th century by Russell Sage and others, writing:

> One of the most striking characteristics of the English money market...is the great part played by "forward transactions — in other words, futures." The use of options or privileges, known to us as puts and calls, is common on the London Stock Exchange. Copper, silver, and numerous other commodities are bought and sold for future delivery. Future transactions in foreign exchange are common. With us, on the other hand, this tendency has been strongly in the direction of spot transactions, the grain and cotton markets furnishing perhaps the most notable exceptions.[7]

Nothing came of Arthur's suggestion for what would have amounted to an organized financial futures market. His idea came to fruition almost six decades later when such instruments were traded on the Street in a more formal fashion, with Salomon Brothers one of the leading players. As it was, the firm became an important force in this area in the 1920s when the instruments grew in importance. They collapsed early in the next decade as international trade fell victim to the Great Depression.

Prosperity returned to the economy after the brief post-war depression. The firm expanded in 1921. In the next two years branch offices were opened in Boston and Chicago, and later in the decade operations were extended to Philadelphia, Minneapolis, and Cleveland. The firm also opened an office at Fifth Avenue and 57th Street so as to be closer to the uptown banks.

Even before the expansion, the Pine Street facility had become greatly overcrowded, and Arthur believed a more prestigious location would better serve the firm's interests and also provide it with a symbol of success. On April 19, 1922, Salomon Brothers & Hutzler moved to new quarters at 60 Wall Street, taking over space formerly occupied by the Metropolitan Bank. It was a decided improvement over the situation on Pine Street. The back-office work was performed

Business expanded, the firm became a primary dealer in U.S. government securities, and in 1922 it moved to more prestigious quarters at 60 Wall Street.

on the second floor of the building, while the traders and salesmen worked out of a large room on the third.

The firm's activities finally captured the favorable attention of J.P. Morgan and other Establishment investment bankers in the early 1920s. Salomon was allowed to participate in several of their syndications — but only in a very small way. For example, Morgan might underwrite a $5 million corporate issue, and send a messenger to Salomon saying his firm could take $25,000 or so of it. Arthur would leap at the opportunity, realizing that any opening of this kind would greatly benefit the firm in its future dealings.

Though only 38 years old when the war ended, Arthur was perceived as one of the district's "coming men." He wrote articles on finance for the general and specialized journals, and enjoyed a reputation for having a keen sense of the market. "He lived the firm," recalled one of his early employees, and he found it difficult to concentrate for long on anything not related to business. Arthur rarely took vacations and those he did go on were short.

He decided to take up golf as a distraction, but was often unable to concentrate on the game. According to one associate, "His [Arthur's] mind — he had a trigger mind. A computer mind. He was always ahead of it. You'd go to hit a golf ball — all our accounts had numbers — 89 was the Chase Bank — and as you'd be hitting your ball, he'd say, 'Say, what did we do with 89 today?' On the golf course!"[8]

"A.K. was a bundle of nerves," said another associate. He generally had little time for pleasantries, and possessed a fiery temper. Arthur would fire associates in the morning and then hire them back with a raise in the afternoon. "He wouldn't eat lunch," remarked a future partner when discussing Arthur's whirlwind activities, "He'd inhale it."[9]

In the early 1920s, Salomon Brothers & Hutzler had 30 to 40 traders and salesmen, most of whom were active in the bond market. While distinctions between these traders and salesmen existed then, they were not as significant as would later be the case. Generally speaking, however, traders would jump in and out of positions, their attention drawn to wherever the action happened to be at a particular time. In contrast, the salesmen had to cultivate their clients over long periods of time, learning their values, likes and dislikes, objectives, and prejudices. Traders knew the markets; salesmen not only needed such knowledge, but also had to possess a finer social sense.

Moreover, their outlooks differed. By the very nature of his occupation the trader was only concerned with the performance of his desk and that of the firm as a whole. In contrast, the salesman had to interest himself with the well-being of his clients, for only by helping them perform well could he hope to obtain additional business for Salomon Brothers & Hutzler. Arthur set the tone in this area as in virtually all the others, inculcating into his salesmen the need to place the well-being of the clients above all other considerations. A deep and full commitment to clients was one of the most important hallmarks of the firm in the 1920s, as it is today in the 1980s.

In this period the traders usually remained in the office at their telephones, buying and selling for the firm's account. Their task was to get in and out of positions nimbly enough to turn profits. In those days the traders tried to maintain as small a position as possible so as to safeguard the firm's capital. As the firm expanded, this became a less important consideration, and in recent years Salomon Brothers has become famous for taking large positions when the situations and customer requirements demand it.

Salesmen functioned much as the Salomons had in the pre-war period. They would make the rounds of the banks, trusts, and insurance firms, creating and maintaining contacts, learning of the clients' needs, and offering them bonds from the firm's inventory. Occasionally the salesmen worked from their desks, just as traders could leave the office when the need arose.

Nonetheless, in the early 1920s the two roles were virtually interchangeable. Charles Simon, who joined the firm as an office boy in 1930 and proceeded to go into sales, observed that a trader who had a position in bonds might try to sell them to clients. By the same token, salesmen could buy and sell when the occasion demanded. Also, a principle of training by exposure was begun which is still at the heart of the numerically much larger training process today.

As Simon observed:

Many of our salesmen were great traders. Many of our traders were great salesmen. Many of our salesmen led the traders into making a trade, and many of our traders trained the best salesmen we had by having them on their trading desk for a year or two so that the young men became hardened....Out of this came an understanding of the money markets that could never be taught by rote or books or lectures. You just have to be brought up as part of it. And the way to train salesmen is to have them on the trading desk for long periods of time.[10]

Charles J. Simon

The need for this close coordination became very important as a result of both old and new forces at work in the 1920s. Of primary importance was the original, unchanging determination to convince clients they could expect and receive superior service from the Salomons. In order to sell bonds to a bank or insurance company, the salesman had to win the confidence of the portfolio manager. He would indicate their quality, maturity, and interest rate to the manager who then would decide whether or not they filled his requirements. After making a sale, the salesman always stood ready to purchase them back at a price close to what their ratings and current interest rates at the time of repurchase demanded.

This presented no problem with government paper and large, active issues, where the spreads between bid and ask often resembled those of active NYSE stocks. Not so the inactives, many of which wouldn't trade more than once or twice a month, and sometimes less frequently. Say a Salomon broker placed $50,000 of a Portland, Oregon, general obligation issue maturing in 1952 with a 4 percent coupon at par. He knew that if money rates remained stable and Portland's financial position did the same he would have to buy them back at around the same price when and if the customer had to liquidate — even though there was no current bid and ask on the Street.

To do this the salesman would have to either seek another customer for the bonds or coordinate activities with a trader, who would take the bonds and trade them for the firm. Morton Webster asserted, "There was nobody exactly like us. There were plenty of big bond firms with plenty of money, but they wouldn't do what Salomon would do — make a market....Salomon was the place where you could call up if you wanted to sell 50 Public Service of New Jersey 3⅝s or something like that. Salomon would make a bid. Other firms would laugh at you." Abraham Eller, a future Salomon partner who went through the process during the 1920s, observed:

> Now these fellows [traders] that sit there at the desk have to have the feel of the market. They are dealing with other dealers all the time as well as with customers. So they know what's going on — or they should know what's going on — they should be well-posted, should have the feel of the market — and they're the ones who make the decision what they should buy and at what price, and what they should sell and at what price. So when they buy something and they want to sell it, they have to promulgate that information immediately to all the salesmen. To let them know what they have to sell. Or, if they want to buy something, they might say to a salesman, "I'm looking for 50 Quebecs"

or "I'm looking for 100 Canada 5s — do you know anybody that's got them?" So the salesman has to have a record of what he's sold and bought....If working properly, the two complement each other. One can't do a good job without the help of the other.[11]

Salesmen and traders alike operated as principals, not agents, which also dictated methods of conducting business. By "principals" is meant that Salomon's traders bought and sold for the firm's own account. Salesmen sold bonds from that account and, when necessary, purchased for it as well. On occasion, bonds and other debt paper would be purchased with Salomon acting as agent and receiving a commission for the transaction, but this was relatively rare. Thus, earnings derived from the difference between the purchase and sale prices; hopefully, the spread between the two would provide the firm with a profit.

In those days this account was known as "the back of the book." This consisted of both securities purchased for gain and those acquired to accommodate a client. Traders knew that they could win approval from Arthur if they moved some of these latter items quickly and at a profit — or even if they took a small loss. Thus, salesmen would place bonds in the back of the book, and traders would dispose of them. And this was another reason why the two had to operate in tandem.[12]

One new factor in the coordination of traders and salesmen was Arthur's theory that banks and trusts would have to restructure their reserves in the faster moving banking world of the post-war period. Previously these institutions maintained two distinct categories of reserves: investments and cash equivalents. When difficulties developed, a bank, which under ordinary circumstances had a reasonable cash position, might find itself having to liquidate investments at much lower prices.

Arthur believed that in the future these institutions would have to create a secondary reserve to stand between longer term investments and cash. These would consist of bankers acceptances and other short term, liquid paper. Arthur

The firm's steady growth is reflected in this 1922 holiday gathering at the Claridge Hotel. Hosting the celebration are the three Salomon brothers: Arthur (at head

table, sixth from left, with mustache); Percy (directly in front of Arthur); and
Herbert (right side wall, fifth from right, with glasses).

thought these would become a key product for Salomon Brothers & Hutzler. This was a fast moving market, and the acquisition and placement of such paper required much more coordination between salesmen and traders than traditionally had been the case.[13]

Another new technique requiring closer cooperation was that of portfolio exchanges, or "swaps." In these a dealer purchased securities from an institution in order to provide it with the funds needed to acquire a new issue or other outstanding securities. The Salomons pioneered in this now familiar exercise in 1924, when the firm offered to exchange $220 million in Liberty bonds, Treasury notes, and Treasury certificates for a new issue of 4 percent Treasury bonds.

This was a major operation, requiring the close coordination of Salomon's bond dealers and its salesmen. Later the technique was broadened, so that swaps occurred whenever a customer could upgrade his portfolio or obtain even minutely higher yields. The Salomons had to engage in a constant training and research effort to keep up with the many changes in the markets for bonds and money instruments. This was an early manifestation of the ingrained habit of learning more and better methods of conducting business that exists now and will continue in the future.[14]

Almost all of the newcomers were hired by Arthur, who had a keen eye for talent. (He also selected some people who might bring in business through family connections.) All of them were placed in an apprenticeship and, if successful, would capture the attention of one of the older, more experienced men, who would serve as a mentor and instructor. Assuming all went well, they would be given a chance at something better. There was no formal training program, but rather a process of self-education that included listening to discussions among the veterans.

The pay was not very attractive, even by the standards of the time — $6 or so a week for runners and clerks, and $25 per week for starting salesmen and traders. Moreover, unlike virtually every other Wall Street firm, Salomon Brothers & Hutzler did not pay commissions, a matter which so grated on traders and salesmen that some would leave to try to increase their incomes elsewhere. This practice probably derived from Arthur's belief that his traders and salesmen had to function as a team. Placing them on commission could set one against the other, and each would become more concerned with his individual progress than with that of the firm at large. Remuneration policy was a bone of contention at the time and during the next decade, but eventually was perceived as a source of the firm's strength, a practice which made it unique and contributed to its *élan*. Even so, Salomon had ways of improving remuneration. After a man proved himself he might go "on contract," meaning that he would receive a share of the firm's profits; his share would rise with seniority and in accordance with his contributions to the firm.

One salesman of that period, William Morris, offered some insight into the ways individuals made their starts on the Street in this period. In 1922 he met Mrs. Arthur Salomon at a dinner dance and, in the course of conversation, mentioned he was looking for a job. She offered to provide him with an introduction to her husband, and Morris went to see him at the Pine Street offices where the firm was then located.

> So I had an appointment with Arthur Salomon, and I came down to see him, and I said, "I don't know anything about this business." He said, "But I know you'll do well because you've a lot of ability. I'll take care of you and don't you worry. But you must take a course in the back office, and work with the clerks" in what was called at the time the Statistical Office. So I went to work for them, and after six months I got itchy. And I said to him, "I know this whole business, Mr. Salomon, and I'd like to go out and make calls — to see if I can bring in some business." He said, "Are you sure you know all about the business?" I said, "I'm positive." He said, "I'll take your word for it," and I said, "Fine." Just as I started to walk out of his office he says, "I want to tell you something. If you don't make good in three weeks, you're fired!"[15]

Arthur frequently offered Morris and other salesmen advice based on his experiences. Some of his trading maxims were quite familiar: "Don't average" and "First loss is best," meaning that Salomon Brothers should be quick to cut losses. He also offered suggestions on how to work with clients. Much of the wisdom he imparted was concerned with methods of dealing with bankers, down to the smallest details. "Never call on an account on a rainy day," he told one young man. "Nobody wants you coming into their office with a soggy coat and wet feet dripping all over their nice chairs and their beautiful desks. You do something else that day."[16]

Others had similar stories to tell regarding how they arrived and the way they were treated. Herbert Losee began as an office boy before the war, developed friendships with several portfolio managers at Chase, and became one of the first of the Salomon Brothers' bond traders. Abraham Eller, who worked his way up from office boy, was a trader by the end of World War I, after which he was dispatched to Chicago to open a branch office. An office boy in 1918, William Pollock had become a bond trader two years later, and in time became

"The Discounter" helped maintain a family spirit even as the firm expanded to Boston,

the firm's expert in government paper. His brother, Max, arrived soon after, and developed into one of Salomon Brothers' better salesmen.

Jonas Ottens also arrived in 1918, and in a typical fashion. "I had an uncle who was a friend of the head of the loan department at J.P. Morgan. My uncle sent me to this man...who happened to be a friend of Percy Salomon...and told me, 'I'm going to send you over to the fastest-growing firm on Wall Street.'" Like many of the others, Ottens began as an office boy. He then rose to assist a trader, and toward the end of the decade ran the utility bond desk.

Morton Webster, who filled a variety of posts at Salomon Brothers & Hutzler in the 1920s, told a similar story. "Herbert [Salomon] and I belonged to the Woodmere Club and became very good friends....I spoke with Herbert about my coming down to Wall Street — this was in the 1920s and Wall Street was the El Dorado of the world — the money was just flowing in the streets — so he said, 'Come on down

Chicago, Buffalo, Pittsburgh, Cleveland, Minneapolis and Philadelphia.

31

and see me whenever you're ready.' I went down to see him and he said I could start right at the bottom of the cage...."

Rudolf Smutny joined the Salomons in 1919 after military service. He began by taking charge of the firm's original business, that of lining up credit for brokers, but soon after was trained to be a dealer and, when he developed good relations with portfolio managers, was shifted into sales. An aggressive, hard-bitten salesman, Smutny made the rounds of the New York banks two or three times a day, and soon became known as one of the most persistent individuals in the district. Girard Spencer was one of the few college men to enter the firm. He started out as a stockbroker, switched to government bonds, and wrote the first bond letter Salomon Brothers ever published. Jerome Nammack also had been a runner who advanced to sales, specializing in placing bonds at insurance companies.

Robert J. Quinn was taken on as an office boy in 1924. "One day A.K. came over and asked if I'd like to work in the trading room. I said, 'I certainly would,' and he said, 'Send Clem Gaertner [the office manager in the 1920s who later became the partner in charge of operations] in to see me.' So I went to work in the trading room. From position clerk I went to order clerk...and then eventually became a trader." Another trader, David Finkle, was hired as an assistant bookkeeper in 1922, after having worked for a publishing company and a Curb broker; he had friends at Kuhn, Loeb who recommended him to Arthur. Within a year he was at the bond desk.

Henry Rosenfeld's father was an executive at Prudential, an important insurance firm with which the Salomons did a large amount of business. The elder Rosenfeld asked Arthur to find his son a place there, and Henry became one of the firm's more important salesmen during the interwar period. Daniel Kelly was a student who came to the firm in 1924 to work as a part-time runner, went on to assist Hutzler on the NYSE floor, and later advanced to bond trading. Irving Kaufman went from high school to a job as a runner in 1926; his father knew a friend of the Salomons. Harry Brown was acquainted with Arthur's brother-in-law, Stanley Heller, and after working as a runner and clerk for several brokerages went through the familiar apprenticeship at Salomon Brothers & Hutzler. Heller also worked there for a while before leaving to become a Curb broker. Stanley Jacobs, whose father was a NYSE member who knew Arthur, arrived at mid-decade to take a post at the bond desk.[17]

Most of the salesmen and traders had similar backgrounds. Many were either East European Jewish or Irish, usually second generation Americans, with little formal education. "You've heard of college dropouts?" asked William Pollock. "They were high school dropouts, and I belong to a class even lower than that, grammar school dropout." Abraham Eller put it best:

> I think what helped make Salomon Brothers was not only the partners, but that the men they hired were hungry, if I may put it that way. We were hungry to succeed. We weren't the sons of rich men. We were boys from middle-class families. Our families weren't poor, but they weren't rich. So they worked. And we worked. It was fun to work and accomplish something. To see results.[18]

However, there were exceptions. As indicated, Spencer was a college graduate and several salesmen and dealers took courses at New York University, to the point where Marcus Nadler, one of the school's most respected finance professors, was almost an unofficial advisor for the firm. Kelly earned a B.A. and M.A. in history at NYU, and some of the others had a year or two at college before leaving to seek employment in the financial district. The firm even attracted a certified intellectual. In the late 1920s Edward Holsten arrived to handle industrial bonds, and then went into sales. A Harvard graduate who had majored in philosophy, Holsten started a tradition at Salomon; from then on there would be what one of the old-timers called "a ranking brain," a spokesman or at least a prominent figure to indicate that, like the Establishment houses, Salomon Brothers & Hutzler too had individuals capable of discoursing on matters other than point spreads.

Holsten both impressed and annoyed some of the others, who suspected he looked down upon them and was a trifle devious. Charles Simon, who arrived at the firm in 1930 as an office boy and who later, as a salesman, pioneered in selling bonds to country banks, recalls one of his first contacts with Holsten. "[He was] a man of imperious stature who once told me that he'd written his thesis at Harvard on a book called *The Prince*. And I never forgot it, because indeed I always thought he and the Prince were brothers."[19]

Such were the individuals who, led by Arthur, made Salomon Brothers & Hutzler one of the more rapidly growing and innovative Wall Street firms during the Great Bull Market of the 1920s. Business boomed, and there were rewards for successful traders and salesmen. Levy and Losee, who had become partners in 1918, were joined by Harold Cone, who assisted Hutzler on the NYSE floor in 1922, and four years later by Eller and Nammack.[20] Smutny, whose contacts at the insurance companies were growing, was named partner in 1927. Salomon Brothers & Hutzler was hardly in the same class of size and influence as Morgan and the other better-known firms, but it had become a respected entity on the second or third level of the pecking order.

As part of his dedication to serving customers, Arthur approved a tentative move into the equities area. At a time when activity and interest in stocks were soaring, a small number of clients were accommodated in this fashion. By early 1927 the firm had several hundred such customers, and a room where they could gather to peruse the ticker tape and talk with brokers was set aside at 60 Wall.[21]

Salomon's major commitment, however, remained to debt securities, and not much thought was given to expanding into the retail area. Nevertheless, the venture into equities did enable the firm to make greater use of Hutzler's NYSE seat and provided some additional profits. But the move was tentative, and Arthur was ever prepared to pull back. While other houses were plunging into the rampaging stock market, Salomon Brothers & Hutzler moved into it most cautiously, and then with some reluctance.

This seemed prudent to Arthur, especially in light of what he had learned during the stock market's collapse in the post-war recession. Then the Dow Jones industrial average declined from 119 in October 1919, to 66 in December 1920. During the same period the rails went from 82 to 66. The bond average remained relatively steady, however, starting out at 81 and ending at 76.

This was to have been expected. Stocks were for speculators and bonds for investors, and the kinds of institutions with which the Salomons dealt were in the latter category. So the firm did not have a significant exposure to stocks during the bull market, which meant it missed an opportunity for spectacular profits. For the same reason, however, it did not suffer badly in the Great Crash and its aftermath.

By the middle of the 1920s, Salomon Brothers & Hutzler had achieved wide recognition in the district as an

Operations personnel, circa 1928, pictured here in "the cage", where the workload was sometimes so heavy that young clerks would spend the night sleeping on the floor to get an early start the next morning.

aggressive buyer and seller of short term paper. In profiling Arthur in 1924, the *New York Post* wrote: "The Discount House now is generally regarded as something of a shock absorber, providing the machinery for readily marketing millions of dollars worth of banking investments at a moment's notice."[22] Most of this paper consisted of Treasury certificates and notes, Federal Land Bank bonds, Liberty bonds, foreign government bonds, and short term paper issued by industrial corporations.

In addition, Arthur expanded the firm's operations in the equipment trust certificate market, concentrating on the rails. This was not a new field for the Salomons, who had purchased and sold this paper. The traditional way railroads financed new rolling stock was through the issuance of trust certificates, which were collateralized by the equipment itself. In those years such certificates, especially if issued by a large, solvent carrier, were considered quite safe, and were taken up by bank and trust officers.

Such expansion required Salomon Brothers to maintain excellent relations with the lending institutions. The firm borrowed millions of dollars for periods of a few days or even hours. This was not much of a problem in the decade's early years, but in March 1926, the markets turned erratic as the Dow industrial average declined by almost 14 points — the most severe decline since before the World War. The rails had been in a bear market of their own since January, and they sold off on news of the collapse of a proposed merger. This resulted in a short-lived panic and margin calls. Money rates gyrated, disrupting the firm's short term trading. Conditions soon returned to normal, but Arthur suspected the bull market was near its end. He ordered a cutback in activities in mid-1927 and, more important, an end to all margin accounts, thus taking Salomon out of stocks — an area to which it wouldn't return for another quarter of a century.[23]

By 1928, Arthur Salomon was known as one of the very few individuals who could see J.P. Morgan without an appointment. But even this had a negative connotation. Those who were prominent in the firm in that period recall that on one occasion, while Arthur was being shaved, he learned that J.P. Morgan wanted to see him on some matter. He hurriedly wiped the soap from his face and rushed down the street to discover what the Great Man desired. His colleagues at the firm considered this to be a fine thing; even to be so commanded by Morgan was much to be desired. But, in fact, Salomon was still not seen as an equal in the eyes of the Establishment.

Arthur K. Salomon

At 48, Arthur was at the height of his powers and influence. But in late May, soon after celebrating the opening of the Cleveland office, he fell ill. Physicians thought the problem was with his gall bladder, and an operation was scheduled. At the time it seemed a minor matter, for he had always enjoyed good health. Arthur entered the hospital, where he died on July 3, 1928.

There were no obituaries in the New York newspapers. While Arthur had been well known in the financial district, he did not rate such treatment in the general press. Nor was the death mentioned in *The Wall Street Journal*, which in those days was much smaller and less inclusive than today. The most illuminating notice of his passing came several years later, in a memoir by a former client:

> The most conspicuous example [of excellent treatment] was the service the head of an important firm was accustomed to render. On many occasions a telephone call to this firm

brought the senior partner to our office actually panting for breath. He didn't send his "boy," or come at his own convenience — he just grabbed his hat and came. No effort seemed too great on his part when handling our transactions, and therefore it was natural for us to like to do business with this firm, where we felt assured of getting exceptionally energetic service. It was not a matter of personal friendship, social prestige, or any ulterior factor. On a foundation of hard work and intelligent service, this man built up a great business in a comparatively few years. Since he is no longer alive, I am going to give myself the satisfaction of mentioning his name. He was Arthur K. Salomon.[24]

With this, the first stage of the history of Salomon Brothers came to its conclusion. Arthur had taken the firm from a minor element in the money brokerage area to a point where it was one of the faster growing and more innovative factors in the short term securities market.

He had built well. The trading and sales forces were equipped to handle the vicissitudes of the oncoming crash and depression, but not for another generation would the firm enjoy the kind of strong leadership Arthur Salomon had provided for its first eighteen years.

Chapter III

Growth and Conflict 1929-1948

Arthur's untimely death sent shock waves through Salomon Brothers & Hutzler. The partners — Percy and Herbert Salomon, Morton Hutzler, Ben Levy, Herbert Losee, Abe Eller, and Jerome Nammack — were abruptly forced to consider how to conduct business now that their leader was no longer there.

Percy had seniority but was not interested in taking command. Although universally liked, he nonetheless had less of the aggressive and competitive spark of his elder brother. Percy knew his limitations and realized he could never match Arthur's superlative leadership. So he willingly deferred to the ambitions of his younger brother, Herbert, and confined his activities to servicing a relatively small group of clients.

Herbert was confident of his abilities and was willing to contend with the inevitable comparisons with Arthur. For example, long after Herbert's death it was said by a contemporary, "He didn't have what Arthur had. Herbert was a gambler. Arthur would gamble, but at the right time." "Actually I think Herbert forced things," said another. "He always wanted to do business, and as a result he did things without too much thought sometimes. I don't think the department was very profitable under his aegis."[1]

Where Arthur could explode at the traders and salesmen but retain their respect and confidence, Herbert, who also had a temper, was considered by some of the senior men less able in perceptions and knowledge. Moreover, Herbert was an ardent clubman, yachtsman and bridge enthusiast and spent much time on vacation, lacking Arthur's almost single-minded concern for the firm and the district. Typically, he was touring Europe at the time of the 1929 collapse, having delegated his authority to others.[2] Herbert enjoyed food and drink, led a hectic social life, and had no difficulty leaving the concerns of work behind after departing the office. The firm survived under such leadership, but the innovative growth that had been experienced earlier proved difficult to maintain.

In fairness to Herbert, Arthur had led the firm during a period in which the economy and markets were conducive to growth. He died shortly before the climax of the greatest bull market the country had ever known. Herbert took command just months before the 1929 crash, which signaled the start of the century's most fallow period.

Herbert's inability to assume a dominant position in such difficult times was evident and partially understandable. So was the jockeying for position on the part of the other partners, some of whom had natural ambitions for command. Their attitudes and actions help explain the loss of momentum within the firm during the 1930s and beyond.

Morton Hutzler was not interested in taking charge. He was content to remain on the sidelines and take a substantial share of the profits for relatively little effort. Hutzler sailed through the 1920s in fine shape, rarely appearing in the offices and being generally out of touch with developments there. Partly because of this, Bertram Brummer and Morton Webster acquired NYSE seats for the express purpose of transacting business in stocks.[3]

In 1929 Hutzler and the other partners came to an amicable parting. The firm purchased his seat on the Exchange for the going price of approximately $400,000 and announced that Hutzler would retire. The name on the door remained "The Discount House of Salomon Brothers & Hutzler," but this, and the fact that Hutzler remained a limited and very silent partner, was the sum total of his participation.[4]

Two loosely organized factions developed within the firm during the period after Arthur's death and through the 1930s. The basis for the division was both personal and professional, and under the circumstances hardly could have been prevented. In one group were Ben Levy, Abe Eller and Ned Holsten, and the other was comprised of Herbert Salomon, Herbert Losee and Rudolf Smutny.[5] Jerome Nammack was a loose cannon on the Salomon deck, apparently hoping for independent power on his own after both sides exhausted themselves. The traders and salesmen watched from the sidelines, wary of making commitments, knowing the firm's future strategy and tactics depended upon which group came out on top. There was no resolution of this internal conflict for almost two decades, and during that long period Salomon Brothers lacked a definable point of view or even a spokesman.

The division was natural enough. The Levy-Eller-Holsten group included those who were inclined to be conservative in trading, and they became more so during the Depression. Levy, who had risen from office manager to become a trader in government bonds, had the largest capital position in the firm other than Herbert and Percy Salomon. The tall, gaunt, taciturn veteran (who had the nickname of "Silent Ben") was quite ascetic, having few outside interests other than his synagogue and various charities. By temperament Levy was a manager, not a leader or an innovator. He would go through the office during the day, watching over everything. Arthur had been the only other person who knew precisely what the firm's position was at any given moment.[6] Levy had been completely devoted to Arthur, and he did not believe Herbert possessed the ability or maturity to take his place. In reality, Ben Levy probably would have been wary of anyone who attempted to succeed Arthur Salomon.

Abe Eller lacked leadership abilities. He was the salesman who had opened the Chicago branch in 1921. When he returned to New York in 1930, Eller aligned himself with Levy, whom he considered the firm's key individual.[7] Eller appears to have been drawn into the contest due to his position as a partner, and he was uncomfortable with the dissension.[8]

Ned Holsten seemed to be an attractive candidate for the leadership. He enjoyed Levy's confidence and Eller admired his intelligence and education. In charge of the industrial bonds sector, Holsten saw in the collapse of prices the advent of a long period of bad markets, and so favored cutbacks of investments with risk. At the same time Holsten was more flexible than the others as well as being one of the firm's more original thinkers. There was more to it than that, however. A tall, well-built, handsome man who fit in well socially with the Establishment, Holsten might have been perceived as the kind of person capable of opening doors for Salomon in the area of syndications.

Herbert Salomon was regarded as the head of the second faction, but his presence at the firm was irregular, and poor health contributed to this problem. In the early 1930s he contracted a rare dermatological ailment which was almost crippling in nature. For two years Herbert had to live in a hotel, away from his family, under constant medical supervision, alone except for attendants.

In 1932, when it appeared he would never be able to return to the office, he met a German physician who believed a cure might be effected in his clinic. So Herbert went to Europe, remained there the better part of a year, and came home cured. Yet he had to return to Europe for periodic treatments. Due to this, as well as by inclination, he delegated authority to others. Given the collective type of control at the firm, much of his influence was held by Levy.

Rudolf Smutny proved to be the key figure in the group around Herbert. At the time of Arthur's death he had been with the firm for almost a decade. Aggressive to the point where he angered his opponents and intimidated even

Rudolf Smutny

those who supported him, Smutny also was a man of great abilities who, like Herbert, was an inveterate optimist regarding the business. Even those who disliked the man and considered him unqualified for leadership conceded his talents at sales, capacity for hard work and long hours, and keen intellect.

Like Smutny, Jerome Nammack was a risk-taker and an optimist. A partner in charge of railroad bonds in 1928, he had good relationships with the insurance companies, which was most important in a period when business elsewhere was declining. Unable to accept Herbert's leading role, he left in 1933 to become a specialist at the NYSE, leaving a vacuum that was difficult to fill.[9]

Despite this factionalism, Salomon Brothers & Hutzler did not suffer as much as many other firms during the Great Crash. With its small involvement in the stock market, and Arthur's timely decision not to carry margined accounts, it actually survived very well. Indeed, the firm's bond business picked up in 1930, as banks increasingly turned to investments in bonds in the belief they were better situated than stocks to withstand adversity. Not all bond dealers benefited, but Salomon Brothers was clearly one of those that did.[10] This was another tribute to Arthur's early policies and foresight.

Bond prices were firm in 1929-1930, partly due to the initial belief that this collapse, like those of 1907 and the post-World War I period, would be short-lived. In those previous crises, high grade bonds had been a secure haven. Bond prices actually advanced in these years, and did not decline until late 1931. By then, the firm had cut back on its "back of the book" positions, had become more liquid, and had shifted attention from trading to sales.

The situation in sales was promising. The firm's dealings with large financial institutions expanded while the NYSE's dealers withdrew from that market. Prior to the Crash, a good deal of the business in large blocks had been handled in the NYSE's bond room. But the dealers there — many of whom had conducted stock operations as well — had been hurt and their capital depleted, and they were unable or afraid to take big positions. Salomon Brothers entered the breach. By 1940 many banks, trusts, and insurance firms, who earlier had placed bond orders at large wire houses, were doing so instead with Smutny and others who enjoyed excellent relations with the portfolio managers at these institutions.[11]

The markets for international commercial paper dried up as trade declined. In addition, the primary market in corporate bonds was sluggish, since underwriting had declined significantly. For the rest of the decade private placements and refinancings would dominate the bond market, as large

The Dow Industrial, Railroad, and Bond Indices
September, 1929 - December, 1930

MONTH	INDUSTRIALS	RAILROADS	BONDS
September, 1929	342.45	173.78	92.11
October	273.51	159.82	92.71
November	238.95	145.89	94.05
December	248.48	144.72	93.77
January, 1930	267.14	148.86	93.77
February	271.11	152.34	94.12
March	286.10	157.28	95.41
April	279.23	145.08	94.87
May	275.07	143.86	95.25
June	226.34	128.00	94.91
July	233.99	130.95	95.99
August	240.42	131.28	97.08
September	204.90	121.67	97.53
October	183.35	112.50	96.00
November	183.39	105.54	95.07
December	164.58	96.58	95.20

Source: Phyllis Pierce, *The Dow Jones Averages, 1885-1980* (Homewood, Ill.: Dow Jones-Irwin, 1983).

New Domestic Corporate Securities, 1920-29 and 1930-39

(in millions of dollars)

YEARS	TOTAL	REFUNDING	NEW CAPITAL
1920-29	9261	1759	7502
1930-39	4476	2320	2156

Source: Federal Reserve System, *The Federal Reserve Bulletin*, March, 1945, p. 254.

corporations hunkered down, fearful of acquiring additional debt which might lead to problems during another sharp downturn.[12]

Beginning in late 1930, the government segment of the market expanded. That year the interest-bearing debt came to $15.9 billion; by 1933 it was $22.2 billion and at the end of 1936, $33 billion. Salomon Brothers expanded its operations in government paper while cutting back in the corporate sector. The firm's profits fell, and Herbert had to lay off some traders and salesmen, which adversely affected morale.

Nammack's departure from the railroad desk in 1933 set the stage. Since some within the firm credited him with having maintained its good record during the first years of the Depression, this was taken as a sign of worse times ahead. After his departure, several of the older and more experienced people also left for a variety of reasons.

This meant that Salomon Brothers had to seek seasoned replacements from other firms. Ralph "Crackpot" Martin was the most important of these, having come from First Boston in 1936 to take over the rail bond desk. An erratic trader, Martin would blow up in paroxysms of anger when the market turned against him. When everything went his way he would leap to the top of his desk and bellow orders to traders, salesmen, clerks — in fact, anyone within sound of his voice, which may have accounted for the nickname. A perennial bull, Martin had a great reputation for making money during upward sweeps, but to follow him in down markets proved less profitable.[13]

In this period, the firm of C.J. Devine took a good deal of business in the short term market from Salomon Brothers. It achieved this by making better markets and shaving the spread between bids and asks. Devine understood the business, having started out as a trader with C.F. Childs, and he aggressively sought new clients on his own.[14]

During the famous "first hundred days" of the New Deal, Congress passed and President Franklin Roosevelt signed the Securities Act of 1933, which "put a policeman at the corner of Wall and Broad" in the form of the Securities and Exchange Commission. The financial district's Establishment, led by NYSE President Richard Whitney, condemned the legislation and vowed non-cooperation. The Lehman Brothers economist, Paul Mazur, criticized the Act for "preventing long term financing" and thereby hindering the recovery. Sidney Weinberg of Goldman, Sachs said it was "impractical in many respects and unworkable in practice," and similar sentiments were voiced by other Establishment leaders.[15]

The investment bankers were not mollified when Roosevelt named Joseph Kennedy to the SEC, and made him its leader. Their distrust took the form of what was known at the time as the "capital strike." This meant that, to demonstrate that they would not comply with SEC regulations, underwriters refused to bring new issues to the market. Instead they sidestepped the market by selling new debt issues privately to a handful of regular clients.

The strike did not prove to be an unqualified success. Despite it, public bond offerings did rise in 1934, although not by the margin the economic situation demanded. In addition, there was some $3 billion of outstanding redeemable debt which could have been refinanced at lower rates to lower corporate fixed costs and assist in recoveries.

In some cases of inactivity, the strike's impact was incidental, since markets had started to dry up shortly after

Corporate Securities Issues, 1928-1934

(in millions of dollars)

YEAR	BONDS AND NOTES	PREFERRED STOCK	COMMON STOCK
1928	3439	1397	2094
1929	2620	1695	5062
1930	3431	421	1105
1931	2028	148	195
1932	620	10	13
1933	227	15	137
1934	456	3	31

Source: U.S. Bureau of the Census, *Historical Statistics of the United States, Colonial Times to 1970* (Washington, D.C.: USGPO, 1975), p. 1006.

the Crash. Nonetheless, the strike was very much in the news, and was seen as a major block to economic recovery.

Joseph Kennedy knew the district and appreciated its power structure. He had been a notoriously aggressive speculator as recently as 1932, once directing the stock department at the Wall Street house of Hayden Stone. For the first few months in office he concentrated on enforcing the Securities Act with vigor. Simultaneously, he convinced his fellow commissioners of the need to win general support in the financial district. He did not succeed, and the Establishment did not budge. New securities registered declined from $113 million in July 1934 (the month the SEC started operating), to $11 million in January 1935.[16]

Kennedy persisted. Under his direction the Commission's lawyers prepared a new filing form, A-2, which could be used by well-established firms. This new form was much simpler and shorter than the one it replaced. Kennedy alternately wooed and lashed out at the Establishment. In February he said that the financial community was "cowardly and unmanly and un-American [in blaming] the government for its own lack of courage and enterprise."[17]

The Salomon partners were definitely not privy to the ruling circles, and they operated with them only when permitted. However, the firm had the capability to distribute a medium-sized prime issue alone, and to do so would add to its reputation as well as provide needed profits. But this would make it a strike-breaker in the view of Establishment leaders. Such an action would not soon be forgotten or forgiven.

Under Arthur Salomon, the firm had been permitted to participate in underwritings in a minor way, and this had been considered prestigious to the firm as well as beneficial to the salesmen in their work. If the firm acted independently, or in cooperation with Kennedy, the good feeling Arthur had so painstakingly developed with the Establishment would be destroyed. Still, since it had never been a major underwriter, Salomon Brothers was not involved in the strike.

The district was growing weary of the sterile conflict. It was becoming obvious that the SEC was there to stay, and that it was not going to be the anti-capitalist entity warned against in 1933. Several large and medium-sized houses were actually seeking ways out of the strike which would be both face-saving and dignified. The Salomon partners must have been aware of these considerations as they contemplated their opportunities and their risks.

About this time, Swift & Co., the large meatpacker, which at the time was not committed to any single investment bank, indicated an interest in refunding a substantial part of its debt. No record was kept of the deliberations, but it is possible that Holsten took the initiative because he had contacts at Swift, and when he presented the idea to the other partners, they approved further negotiations.[18] These proceeded satisfactorily, and on March 7, 1935, Swift & Co. applied for registration of $43 million of 3¾ percent 35-year mortgage bonds. This offering — the largest since the Crash — was made through Salomon Brothers & Hutzler, which acted as agent rather than underwriter. The distinction was important, for it meant that the firm could offer, as agent, the bonds on a best-efforts basis to its customers at the banks, trusts, and insurance firms, and not take them in the conventional all-or-nothing method. In this way, the firm risked its standing with the Establishment, but not its capital, on the issue.

Swift announced that the proceeds would go to retire two issues of 5 percent notes and bonds, thus effecting a savings for the company. Salomon was to receive a commission of 0.4 percent, or $172,000. This was approximately one-tenth the average underwriting spread for such quality bonds sold prior to the Crash. Kennedy was quick to note this fact, as he did the relative ease with which the offering was organized — 59 pages of documentation had been required under A-2, as compared to the approximately 20,000 pages for an earlier Republic Steel issue before the capital strike.[19] Moreover, the rate was the lowest at which such quality bonds had been offered since before World War I, signaling to other firms the promising investment situation awaiting them if they resumed business.

The Swift bonds came to market on March 27, 1935, by which time the financial district had digested its significance. The reaction in corporate America came even sooner. Within hours of the March 7 announcement, Pacific Gas & Electric

This advertisement is not to be construed as an offer to buy or sell, nor as a solicitation of an offer to buy or sell, any of these Bonds. No person has been authorized to give any information or make any representations, other than those contained in the Prospectus, in connection with the offer contained in said Prospectus and, if given or made, such information or representations must not be relied upon. The offer is made only by the Prospectus, copies of which may be obtained at the offices of the Selling Agents.

NEW ISSUE

$43,000,000

Swift and Company

First Mortgage Sinking Fund 3¾% Bonds

To be dated May 15, 1935 and to be due May 15, 1950

When, as and if issued and subject to approval by stockholders

It is expected that Bonds (which may be in temporary form) will be ready for delivery on or about June 15, 1935 at the office of Salomon Bros. & Hutzler, Sixty Wall Street, New York, N. Y.

Price 100% and accrued interest

SELLING AGENTS

"Underwriters" as defined in Securities Act of 1933 as Amended

DISCOUNT HOUSE
OF
SALOMON BROS. & HUTZLER
MEMBERS OF THE NEW YORK STOCK EXCHANGE
SIXTY WALL STREET
NEW YORK

Boston   Philadelphia   Chicago   Cleveland   Minneapolis

March 27, 1935.

SWIFT & CO.'S BONDS ON MARKET TODAY

Proceeds From $43,000,000 Issue to Be Used for Refunding Debt.

OFFERED BY SINGLE HOUSE

Salomon Bros. & Hutzler Sole Underwriters—Institutions to Be Chief Investors.

Public offering will be made to-day of the issue of $43,000,000 of first mortgage sinking fund 3% per cent bonds of Swift & Co. of Illinois by Salomon Bros. & Hutzler. The bonds, dated May 15, 1935, and due on May 15, 1950, will be priced at par and interest to date of delivery, which is expected to be June 15, to yield 3.75 per cent. The offering is made by prospectus. The securities have been registered with the Securities and Exchange Commission.

Inasmuch as Salomon Bros. & Hutzler are the sole underwriters, the offering involving no commissions to dealers, this issue was said yesterday to be one of the largest ever placed directly with investors by a single banking firm. It is expected that most of the bonds will be taken by insurance companies and other institutional investors.

The issue is one of the first major pieces of financing undertaken by corporations in the country to refund higher-interest-bearing debt which can be called. From the pro-

Salomon Brothers broke the "Wall Street strike" against new securities regulation by serving as the sole selling agent for a $43 million issue by Swift & Co. in 1935.

49

said it would register a new bond issue "in the very near future," and two days later filed for a $45 million issue. On April 1, Southern California Edison registered a $73 million issue. That month $142 million worth of securities were registered, and in July, $530 million. The figure for the year as a whole came to $2.7 billion, four times as much as in 1934. The logjam had been broken; the capital strike was over — much to the relief of Wall Street as well as the SEC.[20]

Sales of Corporate Bonds, 1934-1936

(in millions of dollars)

YEAR	BONDS AND NOTES	
	Publicly Offered	Privately Placed
1934	280	92
1935	1840	385
1936	3660	369

Source: U.S. Bureau of the Census, *Historical Statistics of the United States, Colonial Times to 1970* (Washington, D.C.: USGPO, 1975), p. 1005.

Salomon Brothers & Hutzler had been the real catalyst for breaking the strike. It probably would have ended without the Swift underwriting, for the Establishment lines were already showing signs of cracking. The fact remains, however, that alone of all the financial houses, Salomon Brothers was prepared to take the risks such an action entailed. Some in the district considered the firm a traitor, and this was to have been expected; Salomon wasn't invited into underwritings as often as in the past, and it was accused of unfair practices by the National Association of Securities Dealers, but nothing came of this. Nevertheless, reverberations of the Swift flotation were felt as late as the 1950s, when it was raised in an attempt to block Salomon Brothers' entry into the big leagues of underwriting.

Other firms were secretly grateful for Salomon Brothers' action. Moreover, the success of the Swift sale brought the firm new business; in June, Salomon was the sole agent for a $50 million offering of Socony Vacuum 25-year,

3 percent debentures. This, too, had been arranged by Holsten, who as a result gained increased status and power at the firm.

The Swift operation was considered a bold and innovative step which flew in the face of the Establishment's interests. Yet no one, either at the firm or outside it, seriously believed Salomon was in some way throwing down the gauntlet, or deliberately setting itself on a different path from the district's leaders. However, what was viewed at the time as a specific response to a unique situation might later have been interpreted as a precedent. In bringing the Swift issue to market, the firm was challenging the old ways by which the Establishment conducted business while insisting on developing new techniques which would enhance its position and prospects. Other innovative actions have followed, and this is considered one of the strongest aspects of the firm today.

Under the terms of the Glass-Steagall Act of 1933, commercial banks were obliged to divorce themselves either from banking or investment banking by mid-1934. This radically changed the face of the financial community. For, although this legislation received far less attention than had the Securities Act, it also altered the way the district conducted business.

One by one the great banking houses chose their methods to comply with the Act in ways they considered to be in their best interests. J.P. Morgan & Co. elected for commercial banking. On July 6, 1935, several former executives including Henry S. Morgan, J.P.'s son, gathered at the North Haven Island, Maine, summer home of J.P. Morgan & Co. partner Thomas Lamont, and decided to organize themselves as an investment bank. On September 5, Lamont, Morgan, and Harold Stanley announced the union of J.P. Morgan & Co.'s investment affiliate and Drexel & Co. The statement was brief and to the point:

> A group of partners and staff members of J.P. Morgan & Co. of New York and Drexel & Co., of Philadelphia, formerly active in the securities business of the firms, have withdrawn and are forming a new organization for the underwrit-

ing and wholesaling of investment securities, to be known as Morgan Stanley & Co. Inc. Messrs. Harold Stanley, William Ewing, and Henry S. Morgan of J.P. Morgan & Co., Messrs. Perry E. Hall and Edward York, Jr. of Drexel & Co., and Messrs. John M. Young and A.N. Jones, heretofore managers of the Bond and Statistical Departments of J.P. Morgan & Co., are to be the executive officers of the new corporation. Mr. Stanley will be the president of the new corporation.[21]

Thus was born the central player in the new Establishment, Morgan Stanley, which became a leader in investment banking. Other similar arrangements followed. The investment affiliates of Chase National and First National of Boston united to become First Boston Corp. Later on Drexel & Co. was formed by Morgan's Philadelphia branch; Edward B. Smith & Co. merged with the investment affiliate of the Guaranty Trust of New York and eventually became part of Smith Barney & Co.; Harriman Ripley & Co. was created in part through the dissolution of the National City Bank's important City Company and the affiliation of Brown Brothers Harriman's investment group.

Banks and bankers molded their destinies throughout the rest of the decade. It became common in the financial community for numerous investment bankers and other personnel to leave their offices at commercial banks and find employment at the old and new investment banks.[22]

The Establishment was powerful. The most important firms in 1928 in terms of underwritings had been Morgan; Kuhn, Loeb; Dillon, Read; Harris Forbes; the National City Company; and Lee, Higginson. In 1935 the underwriting field was dominated by First Boston; Kuhn, Loeb; E.B. Smith; Lazard Frères; Field, Glore; and Blyth & Co.

Many of the names of the firms were different, but most of the people running them came from the old group. By 1936, the realities of power in the district had settled back to the previous *status quo*. Morgan Stanley headed the list of underwriters and Kuhn, Loeb was in its customary second

Distribution of Underwritings, 1934-1939

(all figures are percentages)

FIRM	BONDS	PREFERRED STOCK	COMMON STOCK	ALL
Morgan Stanley	25.9	9.2	8.0	23.2
First Boston	12.0	5.1	—	10.7
Kuhn, Loeb	7.7	0.2	4.3	6.7
Dillon, Read	7.4	10.3	1.7	7.4
Smith Barney	4.5	9.8	5.0	5.1
Blyth & Co.	4.3	4.0	2.7	4.2
Total	61.8	38.6	21.7	57.3
Fourteen other New York banks	20.0	29.1	27.7	21.3
Total	81.8	67.7	49.4	78.6

Source: 77th United States Congress, 1st Session, Temporary National Economic Committee, *Investigation of Concentration of Economic Power* (Washington, D.C.: USGPO, 1940), pt. 24, p. 12991.

place. Prior to the passage of the Securities and Glass-Steagall Acts, underwritings had been dominated by just a handful of Establishment firms; the same ones, several in new guises, were still in command.[23]

These shifts and changes clearly had a great impact on Salomon Brothers & Hutzler. The firm had to adjust to the post-Glass-Steagall situation when it came to working with both kinds of bankers. In the past it had been necessary to maintain a good reputation at J.P. Morgan, for example, in order to obtain commercial and trust business and a role in bond and note underwritings. Now the firm's partners dealt with two independent organizations, each with a different kind of business, and Salomon Brothers' strong performance in the commercial area no longer helped to ease the way in underwritings.

Furthermore, the shuffling of people weakened and, in some cases, severed old personal ties that had done so much to maintain fruitful business relations between firms. In the chaotic atmosphere of the times they were difficult to recreate, and salesmen had to revamp their techniques and develop entirely new connections, sometimes with old contacts but at new firms. Moreover, even though the capital strike had ended, private placements grew apace because they were not syndicated. Finally, while joint underwriting activities expanded, the syndicates which did them were small, and were usually comprised of the larger houses from the Establishment.

Salomon Brothers was one of the others in the underwriting areas. The firm was obliged to concentrate upon trading, marketing foreign bonds, the government business, and institutional sales. This return to earlier operations did not mean that the firm was incapable of underwriting. Rather, its activities were less than its growing reputation and placement power might have dictated. While it was true that Morgan Stanley started out with capital of $7.5 million in 1935, around three times that of Salomon Brothers, it was social cachet rather than financial power that enabled it to obtain business which was denied Salomon. Charles Simon noted this gap and the way it affected business:

> The reasons were: if you played golf with Joe Jones of X & Co., one of the fine investment banking houses, and you had gone to Harvard with him and you played on the same ball club, and you were members of the same club — let's say between Yale and Harvard, Deke or the Hasty Pudding — and then he became an investment banker and you became the owner of your company, where do you suppose you'd go to sell your bond issue? . . . . And you don't break such ties until these people die from old age and younger men have come along who have to prove themselves by doing a better job to get ahead.[24]

After a quarter of a century in the district, Salomon Brothers & Hutzler still wasn't even a junior member of the Establishment. Even then it was evident that one or more of three different developments would have to take place if the firm were to make an important move into underwritings. The Establishment would have to alter its perception of Salomon Brothers, or the markets would have to be transformed, or Salomon would be obliged to risk a confrontation with the leaders. All of this would take place a generation later, but even then the firm was prepared to accept the enmity of the district's leaders, as was evidenced by the Swift offering.

An example of Salomon Brothers' willingness to meet competition came when Halsey Stuart, the leading Chicago investment banker, started a campaign to oblige public utilities to accept open bidding for their bonds. This was a sore point on Wall Street. Harold Stuart had been the banker for the Samuel Insull utilities empire in the 1920s, and at that time had issued a direct challenge to New York in both that industry and underwriting in general. In response, the Morgan interests had organized the United Corporation, precipitating a major struggle which only came to an end with the 1929 crash.[25]

Casting about for allies, in the late 1930s Halsey Stuart approached Salomon Brothers & Hutzler, which agreed to offer limited support. Henry Rosenfeld testified before congressional committees and the SEC in favor of the Halsey Stuart position. Since the statement of his position came on the heels of the Swift underwriting, the firm was even more of a pariah in the eyes of some Establishment figures. However, it also led to some benefits, as Salomon Brothers became a junior partner in a number of syndicates headed by the Chicago-based firm. (The struggle was resolved in 1941, when competitive bidding became mandatory, but by then it was a moot point, as war-related needs dominated financing.) Nonetheless, on balance the firm lost business because of its position.[26]

Such was the nature of things in 1935-37. As it turned out, the loss of much of the underwriting business was fortunate, especially during the bear market of 1937-38, when the Dow Jones industrial average fell from 190 in August 1937, to a bottom of 99 seven months later, and the bond index went from 101 to 83. Several major investment banks, including Morgan Stanley; Kuhn, Loeb; and Goldman, Sachs were unable to market bond offerings to which they were committed.[27] Shock waves were felt throughout the industry, as the leaders now sought to enlarge their syndicates so as to spread the risk. Salomon Brothers received a small share of this, but underwriting was still looked upon as a peripheral part of its operations.

The small gain in participations was offset by a major setback. Ralph Martin, by now a partner, was convinced not only that high quality bonds would hold firm, but that they were in for an advance, not unlike what had transpired from 1929 to 1931. He plunged Salomon Brothers into the market. He was wrong; bonds declined sharply, falling from Dow 105 in December 1936, to 83 in March 1937. The firm lost between $1.5 and $2 million. This was nearly half the firm's capital, and one of its greatest setbacks. Herbert was forced to cut back across the line, and he ordered traders to maintain smaller positions. There was no year-end distribution to the partners that year, and all salaries were reduced by 20 percent.[28]

Martin departed soon after, and it took years before Salomon Brothers was back to where it had been in 1936. As was to have been expected, this episode increased the influence of the firm's more conservative element, and of Ben Levy in particular.

Despite this experience, Salomon Brothers did not reform its practices and operations so as to increase the firm's capital. Bonuses were restored the following year, and a substantial portion of the profits was again distributed to the partners. This left only sufficient funds in the capital pool to continue operations, with little left for expansion.

Such generous distributions had been the practice in Arthur's period. Profits were growing rapidly then, and Salomon Brothers could afford both large payouts and expansion. During the Great Depression the partners saw little chance of a return to the kind of markets of that earlier halcyon period, and no one objected to the depletion of capital, even after the Martin fiasco. This suggests that the individual partners were doing better than the firm as a whole.

The coming of World War II had a negative impact on Salomon Brothers & Hutzler. The firm's leaders believed that rates would rise sharply as the need for financing the military program developed. Therefore, they sold long term obligations from the portfolio and purchased shorter ones and Treasury notes and bills. But the Treasury and Federal Reserve cooperated to keep government rates low, while sharply increased railroad profits caused an impressive bull market in those bonds. Thus, Salomon Brothers missed an opportunity to recoup the losses suffered from Martin's miscalculation.[29]

The industrial bond business dried up during World War II, and refinancings accounted for most of the business. America's large corporations, which had striven for solvency during the Great Depression, were now loath to borrow to add facilities which might have to be abandoned once war-related orders came to an end. During this period corporations drew upon reserves and profits to finance expansion. When they needed additional capital they tended to borrow from the government. They often could obtain lower interest rates and faster action from Uncle Sam, and were not troubled by unsold and undigested securities, as might have been the case on Wall Street. Government construction of defense plants and leasebacks were commonplace, as were low interest rate loans for specific projects.[30]

Several of Salomon Brothers & Hutzler's leading figures, including Smutny, Eller, Rosenfeld, Webster, and Holsten, entered the armed services, and Rosenfeld died in

Net Change in the Public and Private Debt, 1939-1945

(in millions of dollars)

YEAR	INTEREST- BEARING FEDERAL DEBT	BONDS AND NOTES	STOCKS
1939	3310	-621	62
1940	2490	-342	69
1941	6011	-125	101
1942	23581	-389	53
1943	63412	-767	-33
1944	64163	-653	136
1945	56813	-1038	464

Source: U.S. Bureau of the Census, *Historical Statistics of the United States, Colonial Times to 1970* (Washington, D.C.: USGPO, 1975), pp. 1005, 1117.

combat. As might have been expected, the firm concentrated on government issues during the war, with Levy, who specialized in this form of paper, becoming its dominant figure.

The government bond business changed as a result of the way World War II was financed. In order to finance the war, the Treasury sold bonds to banks, and then spent the funds obtained from the placements on arms. The defense companies would redeposit some of the money. Then the banks used these funds to purchase additional bonds. In this way the portfolios of commercial banks became major depositories of government paper. The increased capital enlarged the role played by portfolio managers, but also made them more dependent upon investment houses specializing in such securities. Among these, of course, was Salomon Brothers & Hutzler.[31]

In the early 1940s there was great trepidation regarding interest rates. The conventional wisdom held that they would rise during the emergency; however, as mentioned above, Treasury and Federal Reserve actions held them down. In 1944 most economists agreed that there would be a recession once the war ended — after all, such had been the experience after all of the nation's other wars. Moreover, the Great Depression had ended as a result of military spending, and it appeared logical to expect its return soon after peace returned. The experts reasoned that this new recession would mean lower interest rates, and most of the nation's corporations as well as the government prepared for a business decline that was believed to be inevitable.

The decline did not occur. Pent-up consumer spending more than took up the slack. Interest rates rose, only to level off late in the decade. In 1948, when it might be said the reconversion effort had been completed, the economy appeared relatively strong. A brief recession followed, which was ended with the coming of the Korean War, and only then did rates advance again.

In 1948, Salomon Brothers & Hutzler also was in the midst of changes in its operations and was engaged in an internal contest for leadership. Some of those office boys and messengers of the 1910s and 1920s were now partners, and an entirely new generation had arrived and was becoming increasingly important at the firm.

Chapter IV

Search for Direction and Leadership 1949-1957

Ben Levy continued to play his familiar and important role at Salomon Brothers & Hutzler in the years immediately after the war. By 1949 Percy was semi-retired, and Herbert's interest in the business had waned with his health. Because of his temperament, Levy was content to oversee operations and manage the office.

Salomon Brothers & Hutzler had evolved into what was essentially a confederation of quasi-independent traders. Each worked his own desk, uniting with the others when circumstances demanded, and consulting with equals on major undertakings. The salesmen, too, had their own territories and clients, and one salesman's relations with the traders could be quite different from those of the others.[1]

This organization might have been expected to perform well under the kind of permissive guidance Levy was prepared to offer, and it did. But there were weaknesses as

Benjamin J. Levy

well. With such a lack of overall structure, and the absence of strong leadership, Salomon Brothers had to be content with instant reactions to immediate problems and forswear the kind of long-range planning needed to prepare for important alterations in the nation's financial fabric. In his time Arthur had provided such guidance; he possessed vision combined with superb managerial skills and an ability to inspire and instruct his traders and salesmen. Levy could make certain the firm remained on an even keel, but he did not possess the kind of perception and drive Arthur had provided in abundance.

With each man concerned primarily with his own desk and devoted to its interests, there was no one who commanded Salomon Brothers as a whole. Traders might go as far as they dared, knowing that occasional failures would be tolerated and only repeated ones penalized. Upon learning that a trust company or bank wished to dispose of a large amount of bonds, a trader could independently make a bid for them, especially if he knew of potential customers. Several of the traders were engaged in this business during the early 1950s, and when they could not place the securities, they would leave them for a while in the back of the book. Or they might buy bonds for a certain price, confident that they would be able to sell them for a fraction lower and have commissions more than make up the loss. This is illustrative of the way the firm reacted to new opportunities in this period.

In 1949, one man emerged who seemed to fill the role of leader. He was Rudolf Smutny, who still did a great deal of business with the large insurance companies. In that year he offered Equitable Life a desirable package of long term corporate bonds that proved to be very successful. Due to Smutny's skill, Equitable was able to lock in funds at a high interest rate and Salomon made a profit on the sale. In this and other deals, Smutny was recognized as an energetic factor at the firm. He seemed to flourish in the emerging bull market atmosphere, and his influence expanded.[2]

Indeed, Smutny was a perennial optimist on the markets, the economy and virtually everything else. Such confidence served Salomon Brothers well in the immediate post-war period, when the nation was rapidly converting to peacetime pursuits, and a wide variety of old industries were expanding and new ones were appearing. In those years a partner's status was directly related to the amount of business he brought to the firm. Holsten had risen rapidly in the mid-1930s when he engineered the Swift and Socony Vacuum refinancings; Smutny advanced during the late 1940s and the first half of the next decade, when he was a great producer and led the way with innovative operations.

By 1950, Smutny could be described as the first among equals at Salomon Brothers & Hutzler. In fact, he was more than that. His ambition and forceful personality convinced others to follow his direction, even if they sometimes disagreed with him. Furthermore, Smutny seemed to have a clear idea of just how far he could go in pressing others to accept courses of action he preferred. Levy and Holsten watched but did nothing to block him. Then Herbert died in 1951, at the age of 67, leaving the path clear for Smutny to assume command.[3]

Smutny was 55 years old in 1953 and had been a partner for more than a quarter of a century. At that time it was clear that he had become the dominant leader. A three-man Administrative Committee, comprised of Smutny, Levy and Holsten, was responsible for all planning, and the other two were willing to give Smutny his hand. However, both Levy and Holsten sensed that despite his talents, an internal gyroscope that maintains the balance of individuals like Arthur Salomon was missing in Smutny. Furthermore, he lacked another of Arthur's strengths — the talent to inspire loyalty and respect.[4]

The district was continuing to undergo profound changes in the early 1950s, the extent of which only became evident twenty years later. One of the more important of these was the diminished role of bonds in the financial marketplace. Simultaneously came the rise of those large and wealthy institutions — pension, trust, and mutual funds — which were beginning to dominate the markets with their vast buying power. These changes naturally had great impact on Salomon Brothers' operations.

At the same time the firm devoted more energy and effort to equity underwritings, an area in which it had been relatively inactive. One needs a clear understanding of these changes and their implications in order to follow the firm's development during the 1950s and 1960s and, indeed, into the present and future. To adjust to these altered circumstances, Salomon Brothers had to develop stronger relationships with the institutions by offering them analysis and related guidance to facilitate market making.

Reviewing the years from 1949 to 1957, the Joint Economic Committee of Congress concluded that "Compared with the 1920s, corporate financing in recent years featured a higher reliance on internally generated funds, a modest rise in the importance of long term borrowing, and a sharp reduction in stock flotations for established publicly owned concerns."[5]

This analysis seems quite clear in retrospect, but in the late 1940s and early 1950s it simply appeared that activity was stirring on Wall Street and throughout the financial district. Stocks broke out of their two-and-a-half-year trading range in mid-1949 and headed upward. Trading volume in both stocks and bonds expanded, with the former attracting much more attention.

A new, long-lived bull market had begun, and it would last for almost two decades. As always is the case with such

Traders in the early 1950s were busy as a new bull market opened up, eventually lasting for almost two decades.

End-of-Year Closings of the Dow Jones Industrials and Bonds 1945-1959

YEAR	DOW JONES INDUSTRIALS	BONDS
1945	193	108
1946	177	104
1947	181	97
1948	177	99
1949	200	101
1950	235	103
1951	269	97
1952	292	99
1953	281	97
1954	404	101
1955	488	98
1956	499	89
1957	436	87
1958	584	86
1959	679	81

Source: Phillis Pierce, *The Dow Jones Averages, 1885-1980* (Homewood, Ill.: Dow Jones-Irwin, 1983).

a surge, interest at the NYSE and other organized exchanges centered on stocks, not bonds. In fact, owners of bonds suffered in this period. While stocks had their greatest upward move since the 1920s, bond prices collapsed in the late 1950s. It was the first stage in what Sidney Homer, one of the leading bond analysts of the period, would later call "the greatest bear bond market in the history of the United States."[6]

During World War II, the trusts and insurance companies had purchased government bonds both as a matter of patriotism and out of self-interest. They suspected that the country would succumb to a new depression after the war, and they judged industrial bonds not worth the higher rates they were yielding.

The outlook changed with the return of peace and evidence of economic expansion, and in 1945 and 1946 the managers rushed to sell governments and purchase industrials. This often meant that they obtained dramatically higher yields; in this period short term governments sold to yield as little as ½ of one percent, whereas Aaa-rated long term corporates yielded over 2½ percent. Thus, the time was ideal for salesmen skilled in swaps and similar techniques.[7]

Conservative portfolio managers (to their later chagrin) looked upon bonds as prudent, secure investments, especially since the Eisenhower Administration clearly was dedicated to fighting inflation. But these managers rarely made purchases at the exchanges. The NYSE's traders had lost great numbers of their customers to firms whose salesmen visited their customers' offices or contacted them by telephone to take orders. Although competition between investment houses was keen, competitive bidding on bond issues was still unusual and corporate clients tended to remain wedded to their bankers. This was starting to change, however, and a door of opportunity was gradually opening for aggressive firms.

Trading volume on the NYSE, 1945-1959, was a good indicator of interest in stocks, but not of debt instruments. Thus, the real decline of activity in bonds was not as dramatic as the figures and newspaper headlines of the times indicated.

While attitudes toward bonds were shifting, the large institutions had huge pools of liquid assets to be invested. The demands to place these funds strained the abilities of the organized exchanges and provided further opportunities for organizations like Salomon Brothers.

The pension funds were the most important of the major institutions. They had been known prior to the war — some 2,000 of them were in existence in 1945 — but many large corporations did not have them. The ones that did usually invested most of their assets in mortgages, long term governments and highly rated railroad and industrial bonds.

This started to change in 1950, with the General Motors pension fund. GM's fund clearly set the norm for the industry, but, more important, it pressured other companies and their unions to bring similar programs into existence. Within a year some 8,000 new plans had been written.[8]

The funds grew like wildfire, so that by 1955 they had assets of $18 billion, two-thirds of which were in bonds

Trading Volume on the NYSE, 1945-1959

YEAR	STOCKS (shares)	BONDS (par value)
1945	377,563,575	2,261,985,110
1946	363,709,312	1,364,174,150
1947	253,623,894	1,075,541,420
1948	302,218,965	1,013,829,210
1949	272,203,402	817,949,070
1950	524,799,621	1,112,425,170
1951	443,504,076	824,002,920
1952	337,805,179	772,875,640
1953	354,851,325	775,940,140
1954	573,374,622	979,500,000
1955	649,602,291	1,045,900,000
1956	556,284,172	1,068,900,000
1957	559,946,890	1,081,600,000
1958	747,058,306	1,382,200,000
1959	820,296,279	1,585,700,000

Source: *The New York Stock Exchange 1962 Fact Book*, p.45.

and the rest in stock. In 1947 the pension fund managers had invested $2 billion in bonds and $1 billion in equities, and that year they accounted for almost 5 percent of all NYSE business. Moreover, by the 1950s it became clear that equities would play a larger role in such accounts in the future.[9]

It was also significant that while the managers of pension funds purchased some securities at the exchanges, they preferred to utilize the services of salesmen such as Salomon Brothers for bonds, and later on looked to them for stocks as well. The reason for going to the firm to purchase bonds was twofold. First, as has been noted, the NYSE's traders no longer made efficient markets in these instruments. Second, and equally important, was the social factor. During the period between the world wars, bond salesmen counted on family and "old school connections" to sell bonds to individuals and others in positions to give them orders.

Salomon Brothers, which lacked the proper cachet, had to find placements where it could, and these were most frequently with insurance and trust companies. Long before these institutions came into their new prominence, Salomon Brothers had the kind of experience and reputation among institutional portfolio managers that served it well in the investment climate of the 1950s and 1960s.[10]

These same factors were true for mutual funds. The origin of the funds can be traced back to the pre-Civil War period. Closed-end trusts like U.S. & Foreign Securities and United Founders were Wall Street's darlings in the late stages of the great bull market of the 1920s. However, they declined in popularity during the 1930s. On the eve of World War II, there were only 68 mutual funds, with a total of 3,000 accounts and combined assets of less than $500 million. Their sponsors never made a concerted effort to sell them until the beginning of the bull market later in the decade.

By 1950, combined assets of the 98 funds of that year had risen to $2.5 billion. In 1960, there were 161 funds, with combined assets of $17 billion. The larger funds, such as Massachusetts Investment Trust and Investors Mutual, had well over a billion dollars in assets each, and their portfolio managers had become individuals with great influence on the markets. By and large, these new men were products of the business schools, and their family and economic backgrounds were similar to those of Salomon Brothers' salesmen and traders. As with their counterparts at the pension funds, they respected the firm's experience and reputation. All of which augured well for Salomon in the 1950s.

The developing new order in the financial district was coming into focus in the 1950s. Symbolically, it was the time when NYSE President Keith Funston and Merrill Lynch, Pierce, Fenner & Beane CEO Charles Merrill were trumpeting "People's Capitalism" and expounding upon the need to attract small investors to Wall Street. Many of them came to Wall Street through mutual funds. Individual investment thrived, but the institutional forces were growing even more rapidly. Salomon Brothers & Hutzler, which dealt almost entirely with these institutions, was admirably situated to capitalize on the popularization and democratization of the market.[11]

Estimated Holdings of NYSE Listed Stocks by Selected Investors, 1949, 1955, and 1963

(in billions of dollars)

TYPE OF INSTITUTION	1949	1955	1963
Insurance Companies	2.8	6.4	12.8
Investment Companies	3.0	10.9	24.3
Pension Funds	0.5	3.5	24.7
Nonprofit Institutions	4.6	11.7	23.2
Common Trust Funds	0.0	0.9	2.2
Mutual Savings Banks	0.2	0.2	0.4
Total	11.1	33.6	87.6
Market Value of All NYSE Listed Stock	76.3	207.7	411.3
Estimated Percentage Held by Institutional Investors	14.5	16.2	21.3

Source: *The New York Stock Exchange 1964 Fact Book*, p. 23.

Whether or not Smutny worked from any grand design for Salomon Brothers is unknown. His actions indicate he hoped both to expand the old business and to plunge into new areas. In this he resembled Arthur. Harry Brown, who later would join a movement to depose Smutny, conceded that someone like him might have been needed to take Salomon Brothers out of the rut into which it had fallen since Arthur's day.

> There was a time when a very aggressive, knowledgeable man . . . could have provided the firm with greater coverage or business or profits . . . . That was something the firm had not done for many years — hadn't invited anybody in. And also, up to the early fifties, the firm didn't feel that it really needed that much more capital. The firm was content to ride along on that $5-6-7 million, which was ample for the positions

it was taking. The firm was evidently very happy to knock off $700,000 or $800,000 a year to split amongst the 8 or 10 general partners because that was real money in those days.[12]

Salomon Brothers & Hutzler had specialized in dealing with institutions, which meant buying and selling securities for the portfolios of financial and insurance concerns. Trading was an important part of this business, which, as has been seen, grew out of the central operations when salesmen took customers' paper in partial payment for purchases and also as a service to them. This meant Salomon maintained its own inventory, and, while traders were expected to show profits, in the beginning at least their activities were outgrowths of the sales effort.

Smutny was intrigued with the possibilities of trading in other instruments while maintaining the firm's main operations. Under his prodding, the other partners acceded to financing railroad "piggyback" rolling stock and marine containers. Dealings in foreign securities expanded, and Salomon held large amounts of equities in its inventory, contrary to earlier practices. It was implied to the traders that riskier transactions than those countenanced in the past would be approved — with rewards for success and penalties for failure. "He was persistent [and] lived the business," remembered one of his associates. "[Smutny] loved sitting down at the end of the day and adding up the profits."[13]

Smutny scouted for additional areas, and found one in real estate. New York was in the midst of a construction boom, and at its center was William Zeckendorf, the chief executive officer of Webb & Knapp, a $500 million corporation. The burly, colorful tycoon was the dominant force in New York real estate, and seemed capable of taking command of almost any situation in which he became interested. Zeckendorf had grandiose plans to reshape midtown Manhattan. He had engineered the deals which helped create the United Nations complex, and was in the process of planning nothing less than a global real estate empire.

Zeckendorf marketed his first issue of Webb & Knapp common in 1952, and the following year he entered into negotiations to purchase the Chrysler Building, the Chrysler Building East, and the Graybar Building for $56 million. This was heralded as the biggest real estate transaction in New York history.[14]

While Lazard Frères functioned as prime banker for Webb & Knapp, Smutny was able to obtain a role for Salomon Brothers. Drawing upon his contacts at The Equitable Life Assurance Society of the United States, he arranged for the company to purchase the outstanding mortgages and then provide a new, longer term mortgage on the properties. This provided Zeckendorf with the funds needed to complete this immense transaction. The deal was highly profitable, and Smutny's skill in arranging it so pleased Zeckendorf that he called upon Salomon for assistance in subsequent deals. The Equitable was also impressed, and it appeared Smutny was leading Salomon into a highly important field.[15]

Smutny was now considered to be one of the district's most astute leaders, and the attention may have encouraged him to take unwise chances. Within a few years he had also authorized the purchase of additional foreign paper and involved the firm in venture capital programs that put its assets at substantial risk.[16]

In 1955, Smutny accepted a seat on the board of Webb & Knapp, and then took similar posts at Trailer Train and Rail-Trailer, acts that troubled the other partners. There was an unwritten rule against Salomon partners sitting on corporate boards, but Smutny had committed a portion of the firm's capital to Rail-Trailer and Trailer Train, both of which seemed to be shaky operations, and apparently he wanted to be as close to the situation as possible. The partners protested, but Smutny rejected the idea of either leaving the boards or cutting back on the investments, and he prevailed.

That same year the others voted to name him senior partner, and, in 1956, as though to signal his independence, Smutny accepted a seat on the board of Associated Oil & Gas. He had become Salomon's first acknowledged leader since Arthur, and appeared to have the founder's power and authority as well, to the point where he threatened to fire those who tried to oppose him.[17] "To put it briefly," Jonas Ottens said, "Smutny just sort of ran roughshod over them and took charge." "He was stepping on everybody's toes," said Harry Brown, then manager of the Chicago office, and one of those whom Smutny had tried to depose. "[Smutny was] calling every shot in the book. And acting as if he really owned the joint. Well, he didn't own the joint."[18]

By mid-1956 there were tremendous losses on the foreign investments, some of which Smutny had entered into without consulting his other partners. Salomon's capital declined from $11.6 million in late 1955 to some $7 million a year later.[19] In addition, a number of the venture capital deals, including Rail-Trailer, had soured. Finally, Smutny committed Salomon to an underwriting of $160 million in bonds for the Memphis, Tennessee electric system, which had been ineffectively handled. For decades Salomon had concentrated on taking positions in highly liquid government and corporate paper. Smutny had committed large amounts to illiquid instruments, placing funds in a precarious position, and had also compromised the firm's reputation.[20]

Troubled and eager by then to see Smutny go, some of the partners began to think about his overthrow. But who would take the leadership? Holsten and Levy had never shown any sign of taking the offensive against Smutny. Most of the other partners were reluctant to act, perhaps in fear of what might happen to them if a drastic change occurred or the move failed. Initially Levy had remained on the sidelines, opposed to Smutny, but prepared to act as conciliator after it all was over. Then, in late 1956, Levy signaled that he was willing to go along with Smutny's ouster, but would not lead the move. Instead, the initiative came from Brown, Simon and the 42-year-old William R. Salomon, Percy's son.[21]

Bill Salomon had arrived at the firm in 1933, at the age of 19, having just graduated from a preparatory school. A Salomon of his generation would ordinarily have gone on to college, but Bill intended to marry, and Percy was of a generation which believed married men should support their families, not attend school.

Thus Salomon took a runner's job at the firm in 1933 and was soon transferred into one of the cages where the certificates were handled. From there he gained some experience at the trading desks. Late in the decade Bill was placed in sales, concentrating on those large banks where the Salomon name was already quite well known. In time he developed into an effective salesman, trusted by his accounts and respected by counterparts at rival houses. Despite his success, the suspicion existed that he would not have risen so rapidly were it not for his family connections. One newspaperman later wrote, "In short, it would be easy to think of him as another example of Wall Street nepotism and let it go at that."22 Events clearly indicated that this was not the case.

William R. Salomon

Bill Salomon gained experience and insights, and in 1944 he became a partner. Soon thereafter Salomon entered the armed forces, and upon his return in 1946 picked up where he had left off. This meant becoming again a very junior partner in sales, at the time when Levy was considered first among equals and Smutny was preparing to make his move for power.

Bill remained on the sidelines, obviously decent and clearly intelligent, a man whom a contemporary called "one of Wall Street's few genuine gentlemen." He resembled his father more than either Arthur or Herbert, and in the early 1950s seemed destined for a comfortable, respectable, but not necessarily outstanding career at the firm.

Bill Salomon watched Smutny's activities and he also became one of his opponents. Because of his name and many friendships (the older partners had seen him grow up, and took a fatherly interest in his career), Bill had little to fear from Smutny, and so he was free to take issue with him. Bill's opposition to Smutny appears to have been motivated by a dislike at least as much for the way he treated others at the office as for his activities in the investment arenas.[23]

Conflict came to a head in mid-April 1957, when all of the partners except Smutny (who was out of town on a business trip) met to discuss the tense situation. From the first it was clear that a majority wanted him to go. Some thought this too extreme, and wanted to settle for a reprimand accompanied by a reduction in his powers. But the others — Salomon, Brown, Ottens, Simon, and Miles Perrin — insisted on taking a strong line. The meeting became acrimonious, but toward the end all agreed to ask for Smutny's resignation when he returned. After a struggle of wills, Smutny capitulated and agreed to resign, taking his capital out of the firm.[24]

Smutny's departure was noted in the press, but there was no mention of his successor, for the obvious reason that no new senior partner had been named. Instead Bill Salomon joined Levy, Ottens, Holsten, Simon, and Spencer on the Administrative Committee. It was generally agreed that, while Levy was senior in experience, leadership would be collective. However, within a few weeks Salomon Brothers & Hutzler was being led by an informal triumvirate composed of Bill Salomon, Levy, and Ottens. Bill Salomon's role in leading the move to remove Smutny was recognized and appreciated, but the others weren't prepared to accept him as a replacement — at least not yet.[25]

This would come in time, and only after such status had been earned.

Chapter V

Fashioning a Modern Approach 1958-1963

In 1957 Salomon Brothers & Hutzler was a highly respected house best known for its abilities to sell and trade government paper along with a variety of corporate obligations. Indeed, so identified was it with bonds that the district considered a debt to be marketable only if Salomon Brothers was willing to issue quotes on the security. The firm's relationships with portfolio managers at trusts, commercial banks, and insurance companies were excellent, and its reputation in the financial district was secure.[1]

Nevertheless, the future of this house seemed limited by its particular role and financial strength. The opportunities in underwriting, especially, were uncertain. Salomon Brothers had been a factor in this area since the mid-1930s, and did well in deals decided by sealed bids, but it could not compete with the Establishment in negotiated underwritings. There the old-line houses continued to deal with one another, and rejected any others, who were regarded as interlopers. Even had this door been ajar, Salomon Brothers could not have gone through, because the firm's capital was still relatively small. This was the result of a traditional practice of making generous payouts to the partners, and because Smutny had tied up large amounts of funds in illiquid investments.

In 1957, the financial community was just starting to undergo changes which must be considered revolutionary by virtually any definition. The exchange system, the institutional structure, the roles of stocks and bonds, the status of other financial instruments, the methods of trading — all felt enormous strains and had to be altered. Furthermore, the district was suffering from a dearth of talent. The financial community was being led by two groups of people: first, the older men who had survived the Great Crash and the dormant markets that followed, and secondly, others who were proving to be far from the most able of their generation. Bright and ambitious young men did not necessarily look to Wall Street for careers in the late 1950s. It was clear that a new selection of recruits would have to be introduced into the system and quickly trained to take leadership responsibilities.

Finally, the exchanges and financial houses had yet to come to terms with the new technologies symbolized by the computer. They had to learn to understand a world in which information could be instantly transmitted, and masses of data processed more quickly than individuals could readily absorb. A new, challenging era was dawning on financial America, which would bring some to the heights of influence, while overwhelming others who were unable to understand and utilize it.

Few truly perceived both the opportunities and pitfalls of the emerging era. Those individuals and firms which did

Investment Bankers as Managers or Agents: Public Sealed Bidding Issues, 1947-1949

FIRM	NUMBER OF ISSUES	RANK	PERCENT OF TOTAL
Halsey Stuart	104.0	1	32.30
First Boston	37.0	2	11.49
Blyth	20.3	3	6.31
Lehman	18.2	4	5.64
White Weld	13.3	5	4.14
Kidder, Peabody	12.5	6	3.88
Morgan Stanley	11.0	7	3.42
Harriman Ripley	10.3	8	3.21
Union	8.8	9	2.74
Salomon Bros. & Hutzler	7.5	10	2.33
Merrill Lynch	4.5	13	1.40

Source: *U.S. v. H.S. Morgan*, in Vincent Carosso, *Investment Banking in America: A History* (Cambridge: Harvard University Press, 1970), pp. 482-83.

Investment Bankers as Managers or Agents: Negotiated Issues Only, 1947-1949

(in millions of dollars)

FIRM	DOLLAR AMOUNT OF ISSUES	RANK	PERCENT OF TOTAL
Morgan Stanley	1252.6	1	9.39
First Boston	1030.7	2	7.73
Dillon, Read	743.0	3	5.57
Kuhn, Loeb	393.9	4	2.95
Blyth	380.6	5	2.85
Lehman	366.4	6	2.75
White Weld	349.4	7	2.62
Smith Barney	275.7	8	2.07
Harriman Ripley	249.7	9	1.87
Goldman, Sachs	220.4	10	1.65
Merrill Lynch	185.8	13	1.39
Salomon Bros. & Hutzler	88.5	18	0.66
Halsey Stuart	28.8	34	0.22

Source: *U.S. v. H.S. Morgan*, in Carosso, *Investment Banking in America*, pp. 480-81.

were later recognized as the seers and leaders of the new financial environment. William Salomon and Salomon Brothers & Hutzler were in that small group.

Bill Salomon and the firm had to succeed in breaking into the equity area and to develop their relatively small underwriting business. Also, capital resources would necessarily have to be enlarged to provide the wherewithal for such new ventures as well as to maintain the financing of old ones. Salomon Brothers & Hutzler needed a more organized structure to make it possible for the expanded firm to achieve all of this. Additionally, newcomers had to be trained to support and eventually replace many of the veterans who had been there since the 1920s and 1930s.

The need to preserve the firm's working capital was crucial, and achieving that was relatively simple to do. Under Bill Salomon's guidance the illiquid portfolio was cut back, and notice was given of the importance of increasing the firm's reserves. In 1958, the Administrative Committee initiated stringent rules with regard to withdrawal of capital. From then on a partner would receive a salary decided upon by the Committee (initially $25,000), 5 percent interest on the capital he had in the firm, some funds for modest charitable gifts, and $6,000 a year for each dependent. In addition, a sum was provided for payment of each partner's income taxes.

"Even if you did well, you would be living on $100,000 or less, quite modest by standards of the time," recalled one of the partners. "But they were building their capital, which not only helped the firm but also meant that future interest payouts would be larger." Other than that, the partners would no longer receive annual bonuses as generous as they had in the past. "Billy had the vision," said one of the younger men who came into the firm in this period. "He did the one great substantive thing, which was to retain capital. He saw — long before the rest of Wall Street — that capital was going to be the key."[2]

Slowly at first, but then more rapidly, Salomon Brothers' capital increased. Without this, almost everything else the firm was to do in the way of new business during the 1960s and beyond would have been impossible. The decision to retain capital — to sacrifice the present for the future — was to be Bill Salomon's most important contribution.

Bill Salomon also led an effort to expand back office operations and services so that the firm could better meet the changing needs of its clients. In 1960, it introduced a convertible bond service for institutional investors. Other moves were made throughout the decade that initially were impromptu responses to market trends but that later became established practices at the firm. Salomon Brothers was playing a more important role in the financial community, and had to compete with larger and more prestigious firms in the area of services and expertise.

One of Bill Salomon's consistent attitudes was that he intended to make markets in as wide a range of institutional securities as possible. Now that the capital was being built up, he was becoming able to accomplish this. But he knew the firm's loose organization, which had served it well in the past by providing an atmosphere in which originality and innovation flourished, would have to be revamped as activities proliferated and personnel expanded. Means would have to be found to provide better coordination in some aspects of the firm's activities. At the same time, it became desirable to attract more attention to Salomon Brothers' progress and growth, much of which had gone unrecognized up to this time.

The firm had been headquartered at 60 Wall Street since 1922, and the office facilities and methods of operating had hardly changed since then. Work areas were shabby in almost 19th-century fashion, and piles of paper and jumbles of ledgers were features of the cage. This was the time when the major houses and many of the smaller ones, as well as the NYSE and AMEX, were coming to grips with automation and exploring the possibilities of the computer.

Bill Salomon initiated new rules to retain partners' capital, making Salomon Brothers the first major firm to foresee the future need for a strong capital base.

Salomon Brothers, however, was still using pens and manual adding machines to calculate figures at the end of the day. A small cadre of clerks and secretaries, seated on high stools and wearing eyeshades straight out of Charles Dickens, entered bond figures in large ledgers by hand, arranged for transfers, and dispatched runners. Just as they had when Arthur ran the firm, the traders and salesmen arrived early,

Salomon Brothers: Net Worth, 1957-1980

(in millions of dollars)

1957	7.5
1958	7.5
1959	8.7
1960	10.0
1961	11.7
1962	12.7
1963	13.7
1964	15.4
1965	19.7
1966	20.7
1967	22.7
1968	41.2
1969	62.7
1970	59.7
1971	101.7
1972	130.7
1973	122.7
1974	122.7
1975	107.7
1976	144.0
1977	162.0
1978	208.7
1979	228.7
1980	235.7

Source: Salomon Brothers, Financial Statements and Annual Reviews, 1957-1980.

did their jobs, and left after readying their desks for the next day's work. They would leave the paperwork to those in the back office, individuals who often worked well into the night. Sidney Grobert, who arrived at Salomon in 1924 and three decades later was a senior in the cage, recalled many "sleepovers" on one or another partner's couch. As for newly arrived clerks, they would bed down on the floor so as to get an early start the next morning. Newlyweds would plead for transfers so they could live a more normal life.

This situation did not seem likely to change. Most of Salomon Brothers' partners favored financial outlays only when they improved upon sales and trading, and they regarded physical modernization as a waste of money.[3]

Clement Gaertner was then the partner in charge of Operations, a catch-all which included every function needed to support the traders and salesmen in their activities. A tall, white-haired, distinguished looking and dapper individual, Gaertner was held in awe by a generation of young men who arrived as clerks and were broken in at the cage. He oversaw everything from bookkeeping, registration and delivery of securities to the ordering of office supplies. Everyone directly involved would voluntarily concern himself with compliance —making certain that rules and regulations were followed— which is to say that no single individual at Salomon Brothers had that direct responsibility.

Allan Fine, who later rose to a position akin to Gaertner's at a very different kind of Salomon Brothers, recalled their first encounter, when he arrived as a trainee after working for a while as an accountant. Upon being informed by Gaertner that "You'll be getting a lot of overtime here," Fine replied that he intended to work long hours, because he wanted to learn the business and be successful. "I really don't care about overtime, and I'd rather not punch the clock. And you pay me whatever you think I'm worth." Gaertner looked at Fine for a long moment and said, "That's the strangest thing I've ever heard. You punch the clock like everyone else." So he did.[4]

The customers who visited the premises must have been dismayed, but many of the old-timers were proud of their image. They felt that the lack of amenities signified prudence and commitment to the ancient verities. Furthermore, Salomon Brothers did not have a retail business as did Merrill Lynch, Bache, Reynolds and other large wire houses, where it was important to impress investors with the office surroundings. Salesmen entertained clients at restaurants and traders transacted business over the telephone. Therefore, the attitude was, why spend funds on appearances when the same money could be employed in the direct operations of the firm?

Bill Salomon realized that the existing offices and the very informal manner in which business was being conducted limited the house's stature in the eyes of present and potential

Automation was introduced in the back office in the early 1960s to replace inefficient systems, lingering from earlier times, that didn't meet modern needs.

clients. He also knew that the current structure would not be able to support the rapidly expanding firm that he was determined to create at Salomon Brothers.

With these considerations in mind, Bill Salomon recruited from outside of the district for the first time in the firm's history. He sought a person who was a specialist in management rather than an expert in finance. After considering several prospects, he decided upon Vincent Murphy, a 34-year-old Yale graduate who had done post-graduate work at the Wharton School and had worked for the Budd Company and then Johnson & Johnson, where he served as export manager. Murphy's job experience was only in auto supplies and pharmaceuticals, but he was regarded as an outstanding manager and was hired for that reason.

In 1962, Murphy arrived with a mandate to "walk around the place" and see how operations might be improved. He soon recognized the firm's essential strengths and did not tamper with these. But with Gaertner's and Ben Levy's support, Murphy brought the office practices up to date. Books were no longer balanced by hand, and under his direction computers were introduced in a rational manner. Both Murphy and Bill Salomon also recognized the need for more sophisticated public relations. As the firm expanded, greater visibility was required to increase the number and types of clients. With Bill Salomon's initiative, Salomon Brothers employed a public relations firm, Mel Adams and Associates. Mel Adams took personal charge of the account, and began an organized effort to make the firm and its operations better known to both the financial district and the general public.[5]

By 1965, Salomon Brothers' operations were becoming among the most efficient in the entire industry. Bill Salomon was creating the structure that was required to support the enlarged and more complex business that he had sought from the time he had assumed leadership. Institutional advertising and news stories were informing the business public of Salomon Brothers' increased capabilities. As late as 1961, Salomon Brothers ran ads that asked, "Do You Know This About Us?" and then detailed the services the firm could offer.[6] Within a few years such publicity was less necessary as the firm's reputation grew.

In order to support this general expansion, Salomon Brothers had to increase its traditional trading and sales forces. In the previous years, recruitment had been done in a rather casual and informal manner. A young man might have a contact at the firm, or with a valued Salomon Brothers client, or even a district policeman or restaurateur who knew a Salomon Brothers partner, any of whom might be able to arrange a job interview.

For example, Richard Schmeelk arrived at Salomon Brothers in June 1941, to take a summer job as a runner while completing high school. After serving in the Navy during

Richard J. Schmeelk

World War II, he returned to the firm as a clerk in Clem Gaertner's Stock Transfer Department. Schmeelk went from department to department, at one time being like one of the clerks Murphy later saw on the floor toting up profits and losses by hand. He then transferred to the Syndicate Department where he clerked for Theodore von Glahn. In those days the number of syndications was small and Salomon Brothers participated in only two or three deals a month, with little indication of future increases. The district was essentially inactive, and Schmeelk saw little chance for personal advancement. However, when Franklin Grieder died, a vacancy was created in sales. Schmeelk was given the job and assigned to sell commercial paper in Canada, where Salomon was barely represented.

Schmeelk sought to expand the Canadian business at a time when that country was entering a period of tremendous expansion in capital financing. Wall Street in general was paying little attention to this opportunity, and Schmeelk had a chance to significantly expand the firm's business in the North.

Schmeelk worked with the Syndicate Department and was extremely successful in leading the firm to major underwritings for Bell Canada and Canadian Pacific, Quebec Hydro, and several provincial governments, starting with Ontario. Throughout, he was sensitive to national pride, and usually arranged to have Canadian investment banks cooperate with Salomon Brothers. He convinced borrowers that their best interests lay in having an American lead manager with a large sales force and guaranteed exposure in the United States. Soon, Salomon Brothers' activities in Canada were growing faster than those at home. Schmeelk's efforts constituted the true beginnings of Salomon Brothers in the field of investment banking.

John H. Gutfreund

Other innovative newcomers followed Schmeelk in the decade of the 1950s. Some came to the firm in the time-honored way, through a friendship with one of the partners. John Gutfreund graduated in 1951 from Oberlin College, where he majored in English. He then served two years in the Army, and in 1953, at the age of 24, was casting about for a job. His parents belonged to the same club as Percy Salomon, and through him knew Bill, who arranged for an interview with Smutny. That led to a trainee position at $2,250 a year. Gutfreund started in the Statistical Department, and after a few months, when an opening developed in Municipals, was transferred there as a clerk. From that position he advanced to become a junior trader.

In 1962, Gutfreund was promoted to head the Syndicate Department with a mandate to develop that business. He was assigned to the post both because of his record in the Municipal Department and because he was qualified by education, talent and training to lead the way into corporate underwriting.[7]

Although Gedale Horowitz graduated from Columbia Law School in 1955, he knew that he did not want to practice

Gedale B. Horowitz

law and hoped to find a career on Wall Street. A family friend provided him with an introduction at Salomon Brothers, and he became a trainee who learned from experience just as those who preceded him. Not long after joining the firm, Horowitz went into the Army and so was not involved in the controversies surrounding Smutny. When he was discharged in 1958, he returned to the Municipal Department and prepared credit reports for clients. Horowitz was promoted to municipal bond syndicate work, then to dealing with short term notes, until finally becoming a municipal bond trader. In early 1964, at the age of 32, he had become the senior trader in the Municipal Department.

As the number of new employees increased, a training program evolved that was really only an adaptation of the methods first utilized a half century earlier. Whenever a small group of young men about to enter the firm was gathered, they would be put through a period of orientation. This started with time in the cage, where they worked as runners and were thus able to gain an overall view of the firm. After a few weeks they would be transferred to the Statistical Department in order to learn some of the rudiments of that part of the business. The next step was to go to the trading desks, where the trainees would rotate until they found a niche and be given a chance to show what they were capable of doing. Each of them knew he would be judged on the results of his work. "This is a firm of very hard winners," said Horowitz. "You are expected to win. The only time you ever hear anything is when you lose."[8]

Sometimes an outstanding man was hired away from another house by assurances of increased responsibility, challenge, a raise in salary, a chance to share in profits and the lure of working at an emerging financial power in the district. Such hiring has always been rare, for throughout its history Salomon Brothers has preferred to develop its own people, particularly in the areas of trading and sales.

Throughout the 1950s and 1960s, the firm's institutional clients demanded research reports as sophisticated as those being produced by the larger houses, and Bill Salomon realized that a greater effort in the whole area of research was required. It was clear that the fast-moving marketplace did not allow time to create such an operation by internal development alone, and Salomon Brothers first acquired research capabilities by outside hiring. From this base the firm then nurtured its own research facility, which is one of its greatest strengths today.

Many of Salomon Brothers' competitors had long offered to their clients report analyses of bond trends and movements. One of them, Scudder, Stevens & Clark, had a team of bond experts under the direction of Sidney Homer. This group had developed concepts and investment approaches that had captured the attention of clients and the respect of academic economists as well.

In late 1960, Charles Simon approached Sidney Homer and offered him the opportunity to organize a bond market research operation at Salomon Brothers. Simon offered what amounted to *carte blanche* to build such a section. Years later, in his autobiography, Homer wrote: "In a flash I knew exactly what he meant and saw how valuable would be a combination of their unbeatable bond trading and bond underwriting skills and my value studies . . . . The firm backed me up with unlimited resources. Never in the ten years I spent there was any limit even suggested to the costly program of research and publication that I developed."[9]

Sidney Homer

Before Homer's arrival, Salomon Brothers had been known as a tough competitor, but one lacking in research sophistication. Homer changed this. Over his years at Salomon Brothers he rarely appeared on the trading floor and he engaged in research having little immediate application. He wrote several books on bonds, and turned out special reports for clients while working on his monumental *A History of Interest Rates: 2000 B.C. to the Present.*

In time Homer became a partner and the company's spokesman to the investment community. "Homer brings to his field an erudition and scholarship unmatched in Wall Street," said one financial reporter, who added, "He has brought SB&H so much favor that many bond men look upon him as a high level public relations man." There was more to it than that. "Under Homer the research operation expanded, as he attracted many bright younger men to the firm."[10]

Henry Kaufman

One of the prime additions to Salomon Brothers' Research Department was Henry Kaufman. He was the son of German Jewish refugees who emigrated to America in 1937, when Henry was ten years old. The family settled in upper Manhattan, where the father worked for a relative as a meat packer and Henry attended school. After receiving a B.A. in economics from New York University, Kaufman went on to receive an M.S. from Columbia. Thereafter, he took a job as a bank credit analyst and worked towards a Ph.D. in banking and finance at NYU. Kaufman wrote his doctoral dissertation under the guidance of Prof. Marcus Nadler, a semi-legendary figure whose discussion group, "The Money Marketeers," included some of the district's most influential and astute individuals. Several Salomon salesmen and traders, men who in some cases had not finished high school, attended Nadler's classes, and the professor was no stranger at 60 Wall Street. Kaufman, who took a post at the Federal Reserve Bank of New York in 1957 and soon became its chief of research, joined the group, which at that time included Charles Simon.

In 1962, Simon invited Kaufman to lunch and introduced him to Sidney Homer. The two men struck it off, and although most of Kaufman's expertise was in the government area, he was offered and accepted a position at Salomon Brothers. "Henry's first job was to learn the bond business," Homer recalled. "He did that quickly — in a matter of months."

It was a scholar's delight — and Kaufman has always retained the aura of a scholar, an attribute quite unusual for the Wall Street of that period. "This was a group of hard-nosed traders, heavily trading oriented," Kaufman recalled. "But a number of people recognized there was a lot of information being generated within this trading room that was never analytically tapped, put together, and disseminated, evaluated, and so forth. This was not done anywhere else in Wall Street. Since we had enormous in-house knowledge in trading, there were a number of people who felt there would be value added by getting analysis on top of this structure that was generating all of the information every day." Kaufman continued, "At Salomon you don't have to pick up the newspaper to find out what happened. You are part of it, at the hub of the capital markets."[11]

Initially, Kaufman was responsible for credit flow analysis, but soon he was entrusted with interpreting the markets for clients. At the same time he was responsible for monitoring the Fed and through this work became famous. Kaufman's regular publication, *Comments on Credit,* became one of the most prestigious in the financial community and this also greatly enhanced his reputation. Bill Salomon once said the key to Kaufman's success was his "mastery of the art of simplicity." A client, Norman Schreiber, of the financial firm Walter Heller International, observed that he did business with more than 350 banks, and, "Of all these people, Henry Kaufman has no peer in telling us about the availability of funds, the trends in interest rates and their impact on the economy." More than anyone else, Kaufman bestowed upon Salomon Brothers a credibility and renown for its research.[12]

The marriage of the scholar and the traders worked well. Kaufman would chat with those on the floor regularly, obtaining their perceptions and factoring them into his analyses. "Traders are very near term oriented," he observed. "They get excited about something in the morning which by afternoon is irrelevant. So you have to be very careful about how you interpret their remarks. What you want to pull out [of their experiences] is the underlying, meaningful information that exists in the trading room, so that you can give back to the people there a high degree of objective, distilled information that will be of some use to them. For example, the Fed could come in and buy or sell securities for simple seasonal reasons, with no underlying significance. That has to be interpreted to help the trader."

At the same time, Kaufman had to adapt to Salomon Brothers' needs. "At the Fed and in the universities one became accustomed to hedging statements. Here all that red tape is cut through. You can't say maybe, if, and but when you are asked an opinion regarding an action which must be taken in a matter of minutes. What you have to do is push through your mind all the relevant facts, pros and cons, and filter through to find an answer. What you have to do is take all of this imperfect information that is gathered up in your mind, align it, and try to give as perfect an answer as possible." Thus, there were accommodations on both ends. "The important thing is for the academician to be able to work through the existing framework," Kaufman concluded, "rather than to believe that the academician can turn the framework around to his way of doing things." And all the while he rejected the suggestion that there was anything speculative about the firm's activities. "We are not a casino," he would regularly admonish.[13]

Homer forecast the long term trends and Kaufman the shorter ones, and Salomon Brothers had a strong beginning for what became Wall Street's most respected analytical team in the related areas of bonds and interest rates. Most other major research departments were found at the large wire houses and financial service companies. For Salomon Brothers, whose clients were virtually all institutions, to offer such broad research services on so limited a base was at the time unique. The firm obtained an enhanced reputation in the financial community and started to receive the kind of general recognition that it had not received earlier. This not only was recognized by the district, but it had an impact within Salomon itself. "We were no longer peasants," one veteran remarked. "We were the aristocracy, too."[14] But not quite. Competing or even cooperating with the Establishment was a difficult and complex matter. In this period several non-Establishment houses chafed at being denied any significant role in underwriting syndicates, while a number of those within the inner circle believed they were not being given their proper share. During the late 1950s it seemed inevitable that these firms, either singly but more likely in some form of group, would mount a challenge to the Establishment.

The way was eased by two developments: unfavorable publicity given to the Street's leaders by one of the most famous antitrust cases in American history, and the coalescence of opposition around Salomon Brothers and three other non-Establishment investment banks.

In 1947, the Justice Department initiated an antitrust complaint against the Establishment. All the leaders were named in the complaint, although the case was formally known as "The United States of America v. Henry S. Morgan, Harold Stanley, et al." Since there were seventeen of them, the group as a whole came to be known within the financial district as "Club Seventeen."[15] The government alleged that Club Seventeen had acted to monopolize investment banking. That there were informal relationships between the leaders was well known, but at the same time competition between them for clients could be intense. On the other hand, it also was traditional for them to exclude non-favored houses from choice underwritings. Indeed, a number of the defendants — Blyth and Lehman in particular — chafed at their small shares in syndicates, and were outspoken in their contention that they merited a fairer deal than the leaders provided.

The other development was a growing unrest among several prominent investment banks, among them Merrill Lynch, Pierce, Fenner & Beane and Halsey Stuart, which were decidedly not in the inner circle. Merrill Lynch was deemed an upstart; its flamboyant leader Charles Merrill had been a maverick with what at the time were seen as revolutionary ideas on the way securities could be marketed to individuals. Although it was the largest wire house, Merrill Lynch had only a minor position in underwriting, which it was eager to expand. Harold Stuart, the irascible CEO at Chicago-based Halsey Stuart, had mounted an offensive against Wall Street in the 1920s, hoping his city would replace New York as the nation's premier marketplace, and the Wall Street Establishment had never forgiven him for this. He was still at it in the 1950s. Oftentimes a syndicate headed by First Boston and Morgan Stanley would be opposed by another organized by Halsey Stuart. As might have been expected, Harold Stuart was monitoring the government's case carefully.

Judge Harold Medina handed down his decision on September 23, 1953. Not only did he dismiss the charge "on its merits," but he did so "with prejudice," meaning that the government would not be able to retry the case. Emboldened by victory, Club Seventeen's leaders naturally expected a freer hand in controlling underwritings. This did not take into account real and imagined slights felt by some of its members, nor did it give sufficient credence to the ambitions of outsiders. Yet so strong, entrenched, and self-confident was the Establishment that no challenge would be thrown down until it could be mounted as part of a more general assault.[16]

Throughout this period, Salomon Brothers continued to seek additional expansion in the debt area. An opportunity to display its growing placement power arrived in late October, 1962, during the Cuban missile crisis.

At that time Salomon Brothers was a member of a syndicate headed by First Boston, which was in competition with one led by Morgan Stanley, intending to bid on a $250 million issue of American Telephone & Telegraph debentures. This was a huge offering by the standards of the time and considered one of the more important of the season. When the news came of the Soviet-American confrontation over nuclear missiles, stocks sold off sharply on heavy volume. In such an unsettled atmosphere, there was talk of cancelling the AT&T underwriting, and syndicate members either cut back on their commitments or pulled out. Several firms — and AT&T itself — called the Federal Reserve to suggest the offering be delayed, if not cancelled. Salomon Brothers reacted differently. The partners came together to discuss the firm's stance, and on that occasion Bill Salomon urged the others not only to remain in the syndicate, but to expand participation sizeably, to $25 million, or one-tenth of the total.

Such action, Salomon asserted, could prove quite profitable, would add to the firm's reputation for risk taking, and might even open opportunities in other cases. The partners assented, and Salomon Brothers contacted the Fed to urge that the underwriting proceed, not only because it could be handled, but also as a sign to the markets that the group had confidence that the crisis would pass and order would be restored. The central bank agreed, and First Boston was relieved to have Salomon Brothers take a major portion of the risk. Morgan Stanley's syndicate collapsed, and the district's attention was focused on the First Boston group. Many members of the financial community realized that, without Salomon Brothers, the issue might not have been floated.

Three-quarters of the offering was taken within hours, and the news helped turn the equities market around. When the missile crisis came to a successful conclusion, calm was restored in the nation and on Wall Street. Salomon Brothers had been successful, it had turned a good profit on the AT&T debentures, and both the firm and Bill Salomon came out of the affair with enhanced stature.[17]

The crisis served as a prelude to and catalyst for a coalescence of opposition to Club Seventeen, another area in which Bill Salomon and John Gutfreund took leading roles.

Salomon Brothers now desired more important positioning in corporate underwritings, and this ambition was reasonable, given the firm's market expertise and abilities at placements. Gutfreund in particular resented taking secondary positions, and he seized his first opportunity to do something about it. In the 1950s, the State of California accepted open bids for its large offerings, but as a matter of course they were almost always won by the Bank of America. In 1960, however, Morris & Co., a small house with little placement power, shocked the district by submitting a bid and winning the issue. Needing help in distribution, Morris turned to Salomon Brothers and Morgan Guaranty, and they successfully distributed a substantial portion of the underwriting.[18]

Other placements followed, encouraging Gutfreund to expand further, even in the face of some setbacks. In 1962, he approached Halsey Stuart, hoping to co-manage offerings with that leading firm rather than take the accustomed junior role. Gutfreund was rebuffed, even though Halsey Stuart had long and close relations with Salomon Brothers dating back to the late 1930s. Nonetheless, Harold Stuart was not interested in joint management, and so Gutfreund and Bill Salomon had to look elsewhere.[19]

Salomon Brothers, Merrill Lynch, and other non-members of the Establishment continued to be ignored when it came to creating bidding syndicates. Moreover, many smaller firms chafed at not receiving enough bidding opportunities. Throughout the late 1950s there had been talk of organizing a challenge. The talk turned into action in the autumn of 1962, when Salomon Brothers, Merrill Lynch, Lehman, and Blyth united in an informal alliance. They planned to go against the Establishment in competitive bidding.

There is some question as to how and even when this group, soon to be known as "The Fearsome Foursome," came into being. The confrontation had been incubating for

Dinner in honor of two retiring partners given by the firm on October 1, 1962 at Jack and Charlie's 21 Club.

several years, and while the Establishment was annoyed, it hardly was surprised by the challenge. Each participating firm was known for its ability to place securities in institutions. Lehman was an old-line firm long subservient to Morgan Stanley, and disliked the secondary role to which it was limited; Ira Daly of Lehman was one of the prime movers for the combination. Merrill Lynch thought the time had come to expand from its strong position as the nation's leading wire house; Norman Smith led the way there. And, of course, Salomon Brothers & Hutzler was well known for its abilities at trading and placement; Gutfreund believed it had the power to wrest clients from the Establishment. At Gutfreund's recommendation Blyth was brought in; led by Paul Devlin, this firm had a strong identity on the West Coast and was eager to gain further recognition in New York. All were prepared to break with (and risk deeply offending) Club Seventeen.[20]

Of course, there were other firms that felt as "The Fearsome Foursome" did, but that lacked one necessary skill or another. Bear, Stearns, for example, was an aggressive house which, nevertheless, was felt to lack significant placement power. Smith Barney and Goldman, Sachs were not then interested in competitive bidding, thinking it insufficiently profitable.[21]

It should be noted that others joined syndicates organized by the Fearsome Foursome, and each member continued to function on its own. In addition, leadership rotated among the four. For example, in a typical underwriting — of a $30 million issue of 4½ percent Union Electric Bonds in November 1963 — the lead underwriters were Lehman, Blyth, Eastman Dillon and Bear, Stearns. Salomon Brothers took a secondary role along with 26 other houses, while Merrill Lynch did not participate. During this period Salomon Brothers was seldom a leader in financial commitments, for an obvious reason: it still lacked the financial muscle.

Salomon was the smallest of the Fearsome Foursome; its capital at that time was approximately $13 million, while Merrill Lynch's was more than $100 million. Yet almost from the first, Salomon Brothers stood out in the group. "We were joined by almost no one on the first deals," said Gutfreund.

"We made outsized commitments, and were at the mercy of the markets." Mitigating the situation was the fact that there was not much volatility in the bond market during this period. Still, it was a risky operation. "This business requires money and guts," said a banker who worked for one of the other participants, "and they [Salomon] have both plus a very professional feel for the market."[22]

The primary focus was on utilities securities, which were important, which Blyth and Lehman had cultivated and which Merrill Lynch could sell to its large array of clients. Knowing they could place the paper with customers in advance of making their bids, the four were able to narrow the spread to the point where the Establishment was outmaneuvered. "The opposition always despised that," said Bill Salomon later on. "It reduced their cut. I don't think they enjoyed that."[23]

The disruption the Fearsome Foursome caused in traditional relationships disturbed large numbers of investment bankers not directly involved in the contest. Wall Street was and is ever a place where traditions die hard, and Salomon was out to win new corporate clients from their old investment bankers while at the same time seeking additional business from the rapidly growing institutional funds. And the firm succeeded, probably even beyond its own expectations.

The rise was meteoric. In 1962, a year in which Blyth and Merrill Lynch each did more than $500 million in underwritings and Lehman managed $734 million to be the sixth largest firm in the field, Salomon's volume totaled $276 million, which made it only the thirteenth largest. The following year Salomon managed $578 million of underwritings, placing it ninth in the ranking. In 1964, when it moved to sixth place, the total came to $873 million.[24]

The firm had become a major factor in leading underwriting syndications, which now played a larger role in its operations than ever before. It was the most rapid advance ever witnessed in this area; within less than half a decade Salomon had emerged as one of the half dozen most prominent firms in underwriting.

The reasons for this rise were well recognized in the financial district. One competitor described the firm as "ambitious," comprised of "unusual opportunists who want

Salomon Brothers & Hutzler's Underwriting Statistics 1960-1964

(in thousands of dollars)

YEAR	VOLUME
1960	144,204
1961	107,640
1962	275,890
1963	577,608
1964	873,210

Source: *Investment Dealers' Digest.*

to become managers," and "without a peer" in its field. "You've got to respect them for their aggressiveness."[25]

After almost half a century in secondary roles, Salomon was emerging as a major power in financial Manhattan. Back in the 1920s partners there took pride in noting that Arthur Salomon was one of the very few people who could obtain entry to J.P. Morgan without an appointment. While a matter of some distinction, it also indicated a deep craving to be considered at the very least a minor partner of the Establishment. This changed sometime in the late 1950s and early 1960s. The old Establishment was no longer as efficient as it once had been, nor was it capable of the kind of self-renewal the times demanded. It was being replaced by a different kind of power, and those firms incapable of adjusting to the new order would be replaced as leaders by others that could. By 1963 it was obvious that Salomon Brothers & Hutzler would be one of them.

Chapter VI

Change and Expansion
1964-1970

On November 18, 1963, Bill Salomon was named Salomon Brothers & Hutzler's first Managing Partner, confirming a status long recognized within the firm and industry. He had gradually won the confidence of the older men during his six years on the Administrative Committee, and at the same time he had selected and trained a new generation for positions of leadership. The firm had grown significantly. By the end of 1963 it had 19 active partners, 424 employees, and branch offices in seven cities.[1]

William R. Salomon, second generation of the founding
family, rose to Managing Partner in 1963.

The Salomon Brothers of this time had four major sections plus activity in common stock. Most important was the Government Department, which handled bills, notes, and bonds, and was headed by Girard Spencer. The Municipal Department was led by Merrill Freeman. Miles Perrin directed the Industrial and Canadian Bond Trading Department, and Jonas Ottens was in charge of Utilities Bond Trading.

These were the years of the most dynamic expansion in the financial industry since the 1920s. To meet the challenges of this increased activity Salomon Brothers needed trade and sales contingents well balanced in age and experience. In fact, however, it had many older men, a few middle-aged ones, and a small number of young people. It was essential for the firm to bring in and recruit additional younger people for the expanding number of sales and trading positions. This became all the more apparent as many of the founding generation passed from the scene. Holsten died, and Losee and Eller departed. A striking indication of generational change came in 1966, when Ben Levy and two other veterans who had come to the firm in the 1920s, James Carson and Clem Gaertner, retired.

John Gutfreund became a partner in 1963 and three years later joined the Executive Committee. Richard Schmeelk, Gedale Horowitz, Vincent Murphy, and Henry Kaufman also advanced, but time was lacking for the development of enough talent from within. Thus the firm was also obliged to seek experienced and proven people from other firms in the district.

Some of those who were recruited from outside to take key posts became major figures at Salomon Brothers. Perhaps the best known is William Simon, who later served as Secretary of the Treasury in the Ford Administration. Simon had been hired as a management trainee at Union Securities in 1952 after graduating from Lafayette College and completing Army service. He became interested in finance and economics, and proved himself a skilled trader in tax-exempt bonds. In 1957 Simon left Union for a vice-presidency at Weeden & Co., which was a maverick house that later challenged the domination of the NYSE. During this time in his career, Simon became increasingly wary of the Establishment as a result of having competed with it.

The New York Times.

FRIDAY, SEPTEMBER 30, 1966.

Wall St. Partner, 78, Slows Down

The New York Times (by Allyn Baum)
Benjamin J. Levy in the trading room of Salomon Brothers & Hutzler, at 60 Wall Street

By the early 1960s, Simon was recognized as one of the Street's rising men. He was also known as a harsh taskmaster, and a man who put in 16-hour days at a time when this was uncommon in the industry. He would stand at his desk, barking orders to his traders, while gulping enormous quantities of iced water, interrupting his trading from time to time with a hoarse cry of "More water!" that sent a clerk scurrying in with a fresh pitcher. Simon got results, and in the process he attracted the attention of Salomon Brothers' leaders.[2]

Merrill Freeman left Salomon Brothers in the autumn of 1964. A short time later, Bill Salomon offered Simon the position as head of the Municipal Department, together with a partnership in the firm.

Within a few months Simon, Horowitz, and others at the Municipal Department organized their equivalent of the Fearsome Foursome, known as "Guerrilla Groups," which bid on municipal issues. Up to the mid-1960s, the traditional syndicates led by old-line houses still dominated the field. Typically, they involved large amounts of funding, and there were one or two leaders, such as Lehman or Blyth. Behind them would be dozens of houses, each taking a small portion of the issue. This was frustrating for many firms like Salomon Brothers and Merrill Lynch, and for even more aggressive houses such as Weeden & Co. These and several others had the capital and placement power but were not given access to large participations.[3]

In 1966 Salomon Brothers, First National City, Weeden, and Merrill Lynch united to bid on federal housing bonds. These "outsider firms" formed a different guerrilla group for each offering, and because of their capital, their willingness to take risks and their placement power, they could often underbid the more traditional firms. The old leaders were consequently obliged to adapt to the new methods, and ultimately this competition altered the way that the municipal bond business was transacted. William Simon received due credit for this positive change. As recognition and reward for his success, he succeeded Spencer as head of the Government Department when the latter retired in 1967.

The transformation in the equities market was accelerated by the evolving nature of the industry and Salomon Brothers' altered position within it. In the early 1950s, Smutny had concentrated on sales and trading. He had also started to cultivate the rapidly growing group of institutional investors at a time when block trading was in its infancy. In the mid-1960s it became evident that syndication and the placement of large blocks of stock would constitute two of the most important growth areas in the operations of Salomon Brothers.

The change in equities trading began at the National Association of Securities Dealers, whose members were drawn to the market for listed stocks. Traditionally, most of the members concentrated on the over-the-counter market, but starting in the mid-1950s several leading houses made markets in NYSE shares as well. By 1962 they handled some 5 percent of all such trades. In almost all respects, the NASD houses acted as wholesalers to professionals, which meant that they concentrated on the large institutions. Several important NYSE members did this as well, among them Bear, Stearns and Goldman, Sachs. In the early 1960s these two firms had begun to dominate this developing business.

Bill Salomon watched the changing situation carefully. Salomon Brothers had productive relations with many of the same institutions, such as insurance companies, banks, and others. However, these institutions had always identified the firm with bonds, notes, and other debt instruments. Why not transfer that expertise to stocks, Bill Salomon thought, and challenge the others?

It would be a daring move, a break with tradition. Salomon Brothers had been a well-known factor in debt

Partners on the 1964 Administrative Committee included (left to right): William R. Salomon, James H. Carson, Girard L. Spencer, Jonas H. Ottens, Benjamin J. Levy, and Charles J. Simon. Not present was Harry Brown, who ran the Chicago office.

instruments, an area which had been fairly dull for more than a generation. The bull market of the late 1940s and early 1950s had been based on equities. To be principally concerned with bonds in the early 1960s marked one as being stodgy and old fashioned. Now Salomon was moving into an area which was new for it, and more than one person within the firm and the industry wondered how the move could be successfully accomplished.

This new commitment to the block trading of equities sent reverberations throughout the firm. It immediately required an expansion of internal research capabilities and the location and hiring of individuals whose reputations in equities matched those of Homer and Kaufman in bonds and interest rates. It further involved acquiring traders and training others, and all this had to be done in a relatively short period of time. What impact would this have on the older men, who had had no real exposure to this market? Would not failure in block

Corporate Stocks as a Percentage of Total Assets for Selected Institutional Investors, 1962-1972

YEAR	NONINSURED PENSION FUNDS	LIFE INSURANCE COMPANIES	STATE AND LOCAL PENSION FUNDS
1962	46.3	4.9	3.2
1963	50.0	5.2	3.7
1964	52.4	5.5	4.2
1965	55.4	5.9	4.9
1966	52.1	5.4	5.7
1967	57.1	6.3	6.7
1968	60.6	7.2	8.9
1969	60.1	7.2	11.5
1970	60.7	7.7	13.8
1971	67.4	9.6	17.3
1972	73.4	11.5	20.4

Source: Federal Reserve System, *The Federal Reserve Bulletin*, October, 1974, p. A59.25, as cited in Edward Malca, *Pension Funds and Other Institutional Investors:* (Lexington, Mass: Lexington Books, 1975), p.10.

trading have a disastrous impact upon Salomon's impeccable reputation? All of these matters had to be taken into careful consideration in this, the most important diversification since the Great Crash.

It was true that equities were not an altogether unfamiliar area for Salomon Brothers. It will be recalled that the firm did a small stock business in the 1920s, primarily to service clients who were interested in that business during the Great Bull Market, and to take full advantage of Hutzler's NYSE seat. However, Arthur had put an end to this by refusing to operate on margin, and little more was done in equities for the next quarter of a century.

Salomon Brothers made a foray into stocks in the late 1950s, when Jonas Ottens purchased small blocks for clients who customarily had come to the firm for bonds, but were now developing and enlarging their stock portfolios. Ottens expanded this end of the business in the early 1960s, and it became evident that further growth was in store. Contacts were made or strengthened at the mutual and retirement funds. Now other traders such as Bob Spiegel, Ray McGivney and James Keene joined in. But it was still a peripheral enterprise in this period. As Vincent Murphy recalled, "When McGivney crossed 2,000 shares it was a big deal. When he crossed 5,000, there was a standing ovation."[4]

Salomon Brothers decided to become an important factor in the equities market, and for a familiar reason: the interests of the clients were changing, and the firm moved nimbly to meet their needs. As Bill Salomon put it, "Our institutions, which were always interested in bonds, were getting interested in equities." Block trading seemed not only the best way to crack into the equities area, but also one which drew upon Salomon's existing talents. "We didn't have the corporate finance capacity, we didn't have the research capacity," noted Gutfreund. "So how would you get into a market which was institutionalized? You muscled your way in by trading — block trading."[5]

There was another reason for entering the equities market besides client demand. In this period of fixed commissions, block trading was almost irresistible from the point of view of profits. When a firm bought or sold a block of, say, 20,000 shares, the commission was 200 times that of a round lot (100 shares), although the transaction costs were about the same. Thus, a trader might sell a block at a lower price than he had purchased it and still show a profit on the transaction.

Large Block Transactions on the NYSE, 1965-1972

YEAR	NUMBER OF TRANSACTIONS	SHARES (000)	PERCENT OF REPORTED VOLUME	MARKET VALUE (000,000)
1965	2,171	48,273	3.1	1,857
1966	3,642	85,298	4.5	3,303
1967	6,685	169,365	6.7	6,811
1968	11,254	292,680	10.0	12,972
1969	15,132	402,063	14.1	15,610
1970	17,217	450,908	15.4	13,354
1971	26,941	692,536	17.8	24,204
1972	31,207	766,406	18.5	25,284

Source: *The New York Stock Exchange 1973 Fact Book*, p. 73.

Institutional Common Stock Transactions, 1965-1972

(in billions of dollars)

YEAR	VOLUME
1965	23.1
1966	33.1
1967	48.5
1968	67.2
1969	80.0
1970	68.4
1971	92.3
1972	101.6

Source: Securities and Exchange Commission, *Stock Transactions of Selected Financial Institutions and Foreigners, 1973* (April 3, 1974), p. 404, as cited in Malca, *Pension Funds and Other Institutional Investors* (Lexington, Mass.: Lexington Books, 1975), pp. 22-23.

From the start Salomon Brothers characteristically set out to become the most aggressive force in the equities industry, making bids and entering into deals which other houses might not dare to do. Bill Salomon put it bluntly and simply: "We'll buy anything." Moreover, the firm was willing to risk its capital so as to provide clients with desirable liquidity, in effect stabilizing the block market in a fashion that was badly needed.[6]

Recognizing that such trading would expand rapidly, Salomon Brothers again went outside the firm to find talent. Several traders who were experienced in equities and equity-related securities were acquired in the mid-1960s, the most important of whom was Richard Rosenthal. In a period when Wall Street was becoming more attracted to MBAs from prestigious Ivy League institutions, Rosenthal was a throwback to an earlier era in that he lacked the academic credentials soon to be considered indispensable. Rosenthal left high school at the age of fifteen in 1956 to take a job as runner for Ira Haupt & Co., one of the smaller brokerage firms. His exceptional abilities were recognized, and he was promoted to the trading desk. In 1962, Rosenthal transferred to L.F. Rothschild, to become a trader in convertible securities, which at that time were enjoying a vogue. After a stint in the Army, Rosenthal returned to Rothschild and started experimenting with arbitrage as well as continuing his activities in convertibles.

In 1965 Rosenthal was recruited for Salomon Brothers by Bob Spiegel, who promised him expanded horizons and a free hand to develop his talents and ideas. With Spiegel as his mentor, Rosenthal soon became one of the firm's most aggressive traders. "I can't think of a better place to learn than Salomon in those days," he later recalled. "Bill Salomon would give you enough rope to hang yourself — go as far as you could, as long as you were honest with him. So you got to experiment and do a lot of things that couldn't be done at places with a more mature organization."[7]

Others at the firm joined Rosenthal in the equities and equities-related areas, but Salomon Brothers was still thought of as being primarily a bond house and still considered itself as such. However, there was no doubt in the partners' minds that further moves into equities would have to follow. All that remained was to act at the proper time and in the right way. In any case, the initiative would be made on the trading and institutional sales level; neither then nor later did Salomon Brothers consider becoming a wire house on the order of Merrill Lynch or Bache. Nor was it tempted to develop products for the general market such as mutual funds, even though that would have provided a means to capitalize upon their rapidly growing and respected research arm.

This new departure for the firm took place at the beginning of a time of rapid change, which has continued to accelerate in recent years. The exchange structure that had been in place since the mid-1930s was coming apart, due partially to the hectic markets of the period but, more important, because of the inability of the existing organizations to effectively adjust themselves to the changes. Without this radical transformation of the district and its business practices, it is doubtful Salomon Brothers could have emerged so rapidly from its second-tier position. Moreover, if the firm had lacked the aggressive leadership of Bill Salomon, it could have squandered its new opportunities.

The first important crack in the traditional system of equities trading appeared in May 1962, during what some commentators called "The Kennedy Crash." From the morning of May 21 to mid-day May 29, when a selling climax occurred, the Dow industrial average lost 100 points. Then a buying surge began, during which stocks rallied more than 40 points in three hours. Volume came to an unprecedented 14.7 million shares that session, which was the second highest in NYSE history, causing the tape to run more than two hours late.[8]

An investigation followed, which determined that the NYSE's specialist system had failed to maintain an orderly price structure. A study by the Securities and Exchange Commission noted, "The avalanche of orders which came into the market during this period subjected the market mechanisms to extraordinary strain, and in many respects they did not function in a normal way." "Specialists are like all people," one of them told the investigators. "They get frightened." The SEC concluded that "Whatever other lessons may be drawn from the May 1962 market break, the results of this study indicate that both the test of specialists' performance and public presentation of the test results are in need of revision."[9]

In addition, the SEC discovered that institutional buying was largely responsible for the May 29 recovery, with Investors Planning Corporation alone purchasing more than $20 million worth of stock in three days. A number of specialists had been unable to handle such large blocks, just as they could not deal effectively with the rush of individual sell orders. This breakdown prompted two responses: the NYSE itself would have to reform to better meet the challenges posed by this new kind of market, and the rival houses pondered ways to capitalize on the situation. As it happened, the Exchange merely marked time while the investment firms moved swiftly to fill the gap.

Salomon Brothers was a leader in this move, though it had to surmount some difficulties along the way, one of which was the need to acquire more capital. As block trading expanded, it required ever larger amounts of funds, and, while Salomon Brothers usually had enough for worthwhile projects, the commitment to equities meant that the firm had to husband its resources and restrict its operations due to capital limitations. Also, block trading put the company at risk, more so than at any time since Smutny's departure. Salomon Brothers always had maintained inventories of bonds, and almost from its beginning had purchased debt which was placed in the back of the book to accommodate clients. Bonds were not as volatile as stocks, however, and so presented less of a risk.

It is doubtful that the move into equities, as well as other avenues of expansion in the crucial mid-1960s, could have been accomplished without the accumulation of capital that Bill Salomon had initiated in 1957. "It saved us and it made us," Gutfreund later remarked. Without increased capital, expansion and diversification into other new areas would not have been possible, added Horowitz. "It was a business Billy had prepared us for by retaining capital. It was a highly capital intensive field."[10]

Capital, then, was one of the keys, and in the mid-1960s Salomon Brothers still lacked the funds needed to make an important entry into equities. Therefore, for the first time in its history the firm borrowed money to finance a new venture. At a time when its total capital was around $5 million Salomon Brothers borrowed $6.5 million to be used by the equities desk.[11]

Salomon Brothers was not alone in demonstrating this interest in block trading. Oppenheimer, Smith Barney, and others had moved into the new field. And above all there was Goldman, Sachs, headed by one of the district's most powerful and influential individuals, Gustave Levy. His house had a larger capital base than Salomon Brothers and was prepared to make a major commitment to blocks. Bear, Stearns was also in the field, and was led by Cy Lewis, who was deemed to be one of the district's premier performers in this market.

Undeterred, Salomon Brothers purchased seats on the Boston, Philadelphia, Washington, Baltimore, and Pacific Coast stock exchanges in 1965. This enabled the firm to cross trades at these markets when it became advantageous to do so. In concert with these moves, the equities desk continued to be strengthened by acquiring and training more people to staff the expanding equities operations.

The block business was, and remains, one of the riskiest in which Salomon Brothers is engaged. Decisions have to be made in seconds whether or not to commit large amounts of money to purchase a block when there is no certainty that it can be completely sold to clients. Thus, the trader has to consider whether or not there are potential buyers, and also whether the stock in question is likely to rise or fall while in inventory.

Then, too, the Salomon Brothers' block trader often found himself taking risks against the market, purchasing shares when most others were selling, taking on what no one else really wanted. "There is a tendency for everyone to jump in and out of the same stocks at the same time," said Stanley Shopkorn, who heads equity trading, and sales and arbitrage in 1985. "What we often do is sit there, accumulating positions, in an extremely negative environment."[12]

Of course, risk was always a consideration with bonds and other debt instruments, but in the short term their prices were affected more by interest rate fluctuations than by any other single factor. In the second half of the 1960s these instruments were far more stable than would be the case a decade later.

The block trader had to consider supply as well as demand when making his decision. For example, he might decide that a particular block, say 50,000 shares of GE, could be absorbed by the market on or near its current price. He knew that even if in the process of selling the block the price was depressed somewhat, the commissions in this period of fixed rates might more than compensate for the decline.

However, there might be another block or two of GE coming in behind the one he was taking, perhaps an additional 50,000 shares. In this situation the price might collapse, leaving the firm with a substantial loss. It was a fairly common problem in those years, during the maturing of block trading, when such transactions often destabilized the market and called the whole system into question.

For a period of two or three years in the late 1960s, Jay Perry was one of the most prominent traders at Salomon Brothers. He was the subject of magazine articles and was discussed in books dealing with the evolving nature of the securities industry. A native of Hot Springs, Arkansas, Perry attended the University of Texas, where he obtained a degree in English. After graduation he found employment as a registered representative for Merrill Lynch in Des Moines, Iowa. Perry switched to Salomon Brothers in 1964, and was originally placed in the St. Louis office as a bond trader. Four years later, when a vacancy developed at headquarters, he was called to New York where he was assigned to the stock desk and, under Gutfreund's tutelage, learned to trade equities. Within three months Perry was on his own, and starting to make his reputation.[13]

It was clear almost from the first that Perry had a superior talent for block trading, and one observer went so far as to say he "fairly pirouetted around the desk with the grace of a Nijinsky and the single-mindedness of an Al Capone." Another characterized him as being "lean and ferociously competitive," while a third believed him "born for block trading." "Jay Perry's fierce talent for giant trades deals Salomon Brothers a winning hand in the Street's hottest, high-stake game," said one reporter, while another referred to his desk as "the most hyperactive corner in the trading room." Nor was Perry loath to contribute to the image-making. "I'm basically a risk taker," he told one writer. "Taking risks turns me on. It gets me nervous. It starts my adrenalin."[14]

Perry took command of block trading at a time when the subject was a matter of great interest in the financial district. It was to have been expected that major players would receive publicity of the sort that surrounded him. He shared the spotlight with Goldman, Sachs' Robert Mnuchin, who, while less flamboyant, was as self-assured and risk-oriented. He also competed with the calculating Will Weinstein of Oppenheimer and the stars at Merrill Lynch; Bear, Stearns; and other block houses. Contests between Perry and Mnuchin took on huge proportions, and were discussed widely on the Street.

A mutual fund would let it be known that it wanted to sell a large block of stock, and Perry would go to work, knowing Mnuchin was doing the same. Each would alert their staffs, who would get on the telephones to other institutions known to be interested in the stock. Perry worked from a console which gave him direct contact with 120 major funds, and he played the machine with devastating effect. When he had sufficient buying power, Perry would put in a bid for the block, knowing Mnuchin was right on his heels or perhaps ahead of him.

Salomon Brothers wanted both the block and the placement at the institutions, which would enable it to collect commissions on both the purchase and the sale. However, compromises occasionally would be reached. For example, Perry might get the block at his price but be unable to distribute as much of it as he had anticipated, and then he might contact Mnuchin or some other block positioner and offer to sell him the remaining shares for placement with his clients.

It was an aggressive and exciting field, and one which provided the firm with an exposure that previously had been lacking. Equities accounted for a small fraction of the firm's profits in the 1960s and early 1970s, but it was expanding rapidly and clearly would become one of Salomon Brothers' major interests in the near future. In fact, the $6.5 million loan was paid off in three years, and by then equities had become the fastest-growing operation at the firm.

During the mid-1960s Bill Salomon started thinking about a move to new quarters. This was prompted by several considerations, some related to operations, others to the firm's status and future plans. Salomon Brothers had outgrown the offices at 60 Wall. The small firm that had moved there in 1922 with a score of traders and salesmen had expanded more than tenfold and was entering into a period of accelerated growth. During the second half of the 1960s, Salomon Brothers organized new departments in corporate finance, industry and stock research, and international sales and trading, and further diversification was in the works. Additional space was definitely a necessity. In fact, 60 Wall was razed a decade later, and for the first time in the memory of most of those in the district, a vacant lot was left on the Street.

The old offices were adequate for a trading operation but not suitable for a firm which planned to make its mark in many other areas. None of the partners except Bill Salomon had offices, for example, and there was no internal dining facility suitable to entertain clients. Arthur, Herbert, Percy and their successors had no need of such amenities, but if Salomon Brothers wished to enter investment banking on a larger scale, accommodations were required for greeting and entertaining clients. "The partners liked the place," Vincent Murphy recalled, "but clients often remarked it looked like a bucket shop."[15]

Nevertheless, Bill Salomon held back to consider alternatives that might conserve capital, and most of the partners were troubled by the costs of relocating. In the late 1960s most of them received salaries of $35,000 a year plus 5 percent on their capital and the payment of their taxes by the firm, hardly generous by Wall Street terms of the time. This was due to Bill's continued insistence on building up capital, and it was difficult for him to justify moving to new quarters where the rents were bound to be much higher.

The securities markets entered into the last and most spectacular phase of the Great Bull Market in the late 1960s, and Salomon Brothers' business and trading profits soared.

The firm's profits were high and appeared poised to go still higher in the next few years, and this seemed to make the move to larger quarters sensible.

In the summer of 1969, Bill Salomon told the partners that a location had been found where all business activity could be in one place and the partners could be in the trading area at all times. It was at One New York Plaza, then rising at the end of Broad Street, at the tip of Manhattan, just across from the Staten Island Ferry terminal. The building was part of the major redevelopment of the Wall Street area that embraced other projects at Battery Park City. However, its location troubled several partners. Their present offices were a few steps from the NYSE in the old center of the financial district. One New York Plaza was more than a quarter of a mile from the Exchange. This seemed too far removed to some of them.

The fact is that the financial district was undergoing a major geographic as well as structural change. In the future, the exchange system would play less of a role than it had in the past. Block trading and other new activities were eroding the powers of the specialists, and the growth of institutions was dispersing financial power. Bill Salomon was looking forward to the day when the firm and a handful of other houses each would transact a larger volume of business than did the NYSE. In this new world Salomon Brothers & Hutzler would function as a power center on its own, and need not be concerned about proximity to Wall and Broad Streets.[16]

The partners and a number of the retired members of the firm visited the new location in early 1970, peering into what would become their new offices, marveling at a trading area that extended two full floors, and gazing out the 42nd-floor windows which opened to a panoramic view of the harbor. From there one could see Governor's Island, the Verrazano-Narrows Bridge, the Statue of Liberty, as well as Ellis Island and the site of Castle Garden, where the parents of several of them had arrived as immigrants. It seemed quite close by, but the journey had taken the better part of a century.

The firm moved to its new offices on July 17, 1970, but construction continued through the summer and into the fall, and the price of relocation had risen to $12 million. The

Salomon Brothers moved to major new headquarters at One New York Plaza in the summer of 1970; Hutzler was dropped from the firm's name in that year.

reality was important, but so was the symbol. When Salomon Brothers & Hutzler had taken space at 60 Wall 48 years earlier, it had been a minuscule part of the financial scene. "At 60 Wall we had cramped quarters, lousy furniture, inadequate air conditioning, and we felt second class." This was the view of Allan Fine, who helped plan the move. The move was a momentous decision. "At the time no one knew how it would change the firm. What happened was that we grew up. We graduated to the big leagues."[17]

Block trading of equities became a major commitment of the firm, as reflected in July 1970 by what was a Big Board record trade at the time.

Yet there was a price to be paid. While everyone was dazzled by the two-tier trading room and the luxurious quarters, the new place lacked the intimacy of the old. Add to this the fact that 1971 was to be a record year for the firm, requiring large-scale expansion of personnel; it amounted to being reborn, and at a rapid pace. "The place was becoming more formal, more corporate looking," Fine recalled. "We were still a partnership and the people who had been in charge before were still there, but the mood was different. Things got a little more distant. The closeness was gone." To him and others, this was part of the price paid for success. In 1970, Salomon was well on the way to becoming an integral part of the new Establishment on the world as well as the national scene.[18]

A symbolic gesture was made at the time of the move. The house shortened its name on July 17, 1970, thereafter to be known simply as Salomon Brothers.

Chapter VII

National and International Banker 1971-1977

The years from the late 1960s through the 1970s were among the more dramatic and troubled periods in American history. During this time the nation was divided and obsessed with the Vietnam War, which forced President Johnson from office in 1969. Four and a half years later President Nixon resigned to escape impeachment, and for the first time the White House was occupied by a non-elected chief executive, President Ford. America's largest city, New York, fell into technical bankruptcy. The nation and the world suffered through two "oil shocks," which contributed to the disastrous decline of the American auto industry and threw the economy into alternating periods of inflation and recession.

Within this era of upheaval, significant developments occurred that altered the investment scene for the decade that followed. From this tortuous process new opportunities were born for those firms which were both capable of understanding what was happening and bold enough to seize the main chance when it came. Salomon Brothers was one of them. At the beginning of the 1970s it was recognized as an aggressive, ambitious firm; by the end of that decade, the house had truly emerged as one of the district's leaders.

In 1969, the world watched with fear and anticipation as outgoing President Lyndon Johnson battled Congress for a tax increase and other measures to dampen growing inflationary pressures. America's financial woes were clearly affecting the international economy. Chronic deficits had contributed to a weakening dollar. Once the world's most highly valued currency, in 1969 it had become a glut on the market, not only contributing to world inflation but also threatening international trade.[1]

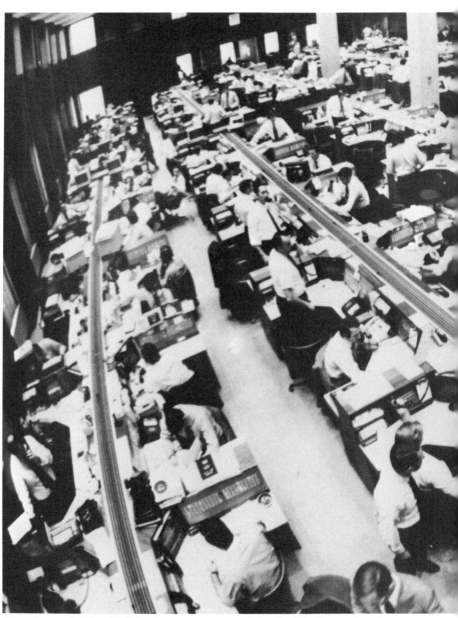

All trading at the New York headquarters was consolidated in The Room, then the world's largest securities firm trading floor, providing Salomon Brothers with

superior market intelligence and distribution capabilities. Seated right center is Bill Salomon, who managed the firm from his desk at the heart of the trading floor.

Some of the surplus dollars in the hands of foreigners were used to purchase gold from the U.S. Treasury. In January, 1969, the gold reserve fell below $12 billion, just $1.3 billion above the amount required to back the dollar. Hoping to quell fears, Federal Reserve Board Chairman William McChesney Martin told reporters in early spring that he would do all in his power to defend the dollar, but even soothing words from the man who was the most respected financial figure in Washington came to little. Finally, in 1971 President Richard Nixon took the dollar off the gold standard. He simultaneously imposed an array of restrictions on imports, instituted wage and price controls, and slashed the budget.

Events of 1973 were even more ominous. While Congress prepared to impeach the President because of the Watergate scandals, the Organization of Petroleum Exporting Countries (OPEC) boosted the price of oil at a time when the wage and price controls in America had already failed to take effect. The nation was in the grip of a soaring inflation when President Nixon resigned. The condition of the economy was being referred to as "stagflation," a combination of inflation and economic stagnation.[2]

The cheaper dollar and high interest rates had a dramatic impact on the capital markets and related areas. It meant that expansion-minded corporate managers who had the option of constructing new facilities or buying out the depressed stocks of companies chose to come down heavily on the buy side. The stocks of capital goods manufacturers were sharply lower than the true value of underlying assets, and these companies became targets for acquirers armed with hard cash. In effect, the decline of the dollar resulted in the creation of a new merger and acquisition movement.

America's economic problems provided opportunities for arbitrageurs who were quick to seize the advantage. Financial activity abroad increased, much of it centered on the Eurodollar market which dealt in dollars on deposit in foreign banks. The floating of the dollar meant that the relative prices of currencies were subject to daily, even hourly, fluctuations, and traders rushed into the market. A bit of good or poor economic news out of one country or another could cause ripples to travel through the international banking system, sending hundreds of millions of dollars from one country to another to take advantage of a few basis points difference in yields. It was a promising market for investors, one which attracted American bankers, including Salomon Brothers.

Many portfolio managers began to doubt the wisdom of banking so heavily on equities. During the 1960s and early 1970s investment advisors thought that a 15 percent return on securities was a reasonable objective. This supposition came crashing down during the decline of 1973-74, when the Dow Jones industrial average plummeted from 1067 to 570 in less than two years. In the same period, money market funds, based on commercial paper and certificates of deposit, yielded from 9 to 12 percent. By the end of 1974 there were some $3 billion in such accounts, and the institutions were rushing out of equities and into both short and medium term debt. The confidence of portfolio managers in equities had been badly shaken, another casualty of stagflation.[3] There was a concomitant revival of interest in bonds due to the fluctuations in money rates. This was a new phenomenon to the generation of analysts and salesmen who had been raised in the post-World War II period.

Now, with rates moving daily, prices of bonds were constantly shifting. Safe medium term maturities carrying double-digit coupons seemed attractive to individuals who believed rates couldn't remain so high indefinitely. Many corporations looked at the relationship between the bond and stock markets and considered restructuring their balance sheets to take advantage of this new financial climate. Bankers who were capable of recognizing the situation and understanding how it influenced domestic and foreign investment opportunities developed programs to capitalize upon it.

From the first, Salomon Brothers recognized that several markets were opening up simultaneously, and the partners moved to enter all of them. One important investment opportunity stemmed from the turmoil in the mortgage market. This centered around the savings and loans, more commonly known as the "thrift" institutions. They traditionally borrowed short and lent long, granting 20- and 30-year mortgages to borrowers, financed by funds deposited by individuals who could withdraw them at any time. State governments placed caps on the amount of interest which could be paid these depositors, and many had similar caps on mortgage rates.

The prosperity of this business depended on interest rates that were both low and steady, as had been the case up to the late 1960s. However, when interest rates rose and the thrift institutions were forbidden to adjust them due to caps, depositors sought higher yields, often in the money markets. Consequently, loan capital for housing became sparse, which was devastating for that industry. The practice of removing deposits from savings institutions to invest the funds in market instruments, known as "disintermediation" (bypassing the thrifts, which traditionally acted as an intermediary between the depositor and the money markets) clouded the industry's future. The thrift institutions had large portfolios of old mortgages granted at rates as low as 5 percent, and had to service them in an economy of double-digit interest rates. The thrifts were thereby placed in a precariously illiquid position, and by the middle of the decade it appeared that widespread failures might hit the housing industry and distress the nation.

It was clear that the federal and state governments would have to do something about this situation, and at least remove those caps on interest payouts and mortgage rates. The mood in Washington and the nation was toward deregulation, which opened doors of opportunity to those who understood the situation.

Another new opportunity appeared in the mergers and acquisitions area. Salomon Brothers had been a peripheral force in this field, but now the firm became more deeply engaged, and within a few years was a major factor. Merger activity also created fresh opportunities for arbitrage, as the Street traded equities, convertible paper and, later, options of firms that were parties to takeovers. With a four-man department, Richard Rosenthal directed arbitrage, became a key figure and, at 27, a partner at Salomon Brothers.

Nor was activity confined to the United States. The growth of the Eurodollar market and the continued revival of Europe and the Pacific Basin created still greater interest in the international markets. For the first time in its history Salomon Brothers organized overseas affiliates, and within a relatively short period of time took a leading position in those markets.

In its traditional bond operations Salomon was called upon to create innovative new ways to utilize and structure debt, and here too the firm rose to the challenge, and in the process expanded its underwriting and investment banking businesses to the point where it became the leader in terms of volume.

These many activities occurred swiftly and simultaneously in America and had a strong impact on Salomon Brothers in the 1970s. So rapid was the pace that even those within the firm who were accustomed to change found it difficult to keep up with what was happening. "At one time it was possible for the partners to know what was going on in all divisions on a day-to-day basis," remarked one of the firm's veterans recently. "Nowadays it is a full-time job just to keep informed regarding ongoing developments."

John Gutfreund had become a central figure at Salomon Brothers under the overall leadership of Bill Salomon. This was due to his experience in trading, syndication, and investment banking. A member of the Executive Committee since 1966, he led many new activities. One of the first of these efforts was in the area of investment banking in all of its manifestations.

Gutfreund and his colleagues were among the earliest to realize just how much the investment banking field had changed by the late 1960s. The role and status of those bankers charged with raising funds and providing advice and liquidity for clients was evolving rapidly. Many of the exclusive relationships that had been common in earlier periods were breaking down. In the past most companies had ongoing relationships with investment bankers which were handed down from one generation of the company to another. In the new, fluid atmosphere, corporations were willing to work with any reputable house that brought them new ideas. "More and more companies don't have bankers of record," Felix Rohatyn of Lazard Frères observed. "On mergers the business is up for grabs — as it should be."[4]

One example of this change was seen in 1968 at Esmark. The successor to Swift & Co., whose debt underwriting Salomon Brothers had managed during Wall Street's capital strike in 1935, Esmark was considered to be a Salomon Brothers client, and off limits to other investment banks by the unspoken rules of the time. In 1968, Donald Kelly took over as Esmark's CEO, and in a meeting with Salomon Brothers representatives he informed them, "You are not *our* investment banker. You are *an* investment banker." He then complained about perceived failures on the part of Salomon Brothers to safeguard Esmark's interests.

The Esmark experience was a shock, but it also represented an opportunity. Salomon Brothers' previous investment banking activities had been limited to a few narrow specialties, and little was being done to expand from this base. The corporate finance operation was still called the Statistical Department, and its activities were pretty much confined to competitive bids in public utilities, rail equipment, and the like. Statistical personnel worked closely with the syndicate desk, which as recently as the mid-1960s comprised John Gutfreund, Herb Losee, Jason Elsas and several clerks. "In those days issues were quite small," recalled Elsas, who arrived there in 1960. "They were infrequent, too. There were only two or three competitive bids a week, and we generally bid as part of a syndicate headed by Halsey Stuart. We were not a manager in those days. Our commitments were generally in the one to one and a half million dollar range."[5]

By the early 1970s, the firm was serving as manager for industrial bonds, and, of course, it maintained relations with a small handful of industrial firms. Just as the Canadian desk under Richard Schmeelk had expanded significantly into investment banking, ways were being explored as how best to do the same with clients in the United States.

Even prior to the meeting with Esmark, the Executive Committee had concluded that the firm had all the capabilities to become one of the leaders in investment banking. Salomon Brothers possessed an in-depth understanding of the market, a preeminent distribution system, a keen and sophisticated understanding of the marketplace, and in Sidney Homer and

Henry Kaufman two of the most respected analysts in the industry. As Steven Grand-Jean, a future partner in corporate finance, would put it, "All that was lacking were clients."[6]

To organize a corporate finance department, Salomon Brothers required an individual with the requisite social cachet and business background to head and develop the program and train personnel, but most of all, one who possessed the ability to crack the old Establishment. As Rohatyn put it, "They have the competence and the capital, but they may have to buy the three-piece suit."[7]

No thought was given to seeking such a person at another Wall Street house. As John Gutfreund knew, "It would have been difficult for our people to accept an organization thrust upon them by someone from another firm on the Street." Instead, the search concentrated on the corporate world, and in 1969 the firm selected Daniel Sargent, a former banker who had gone on to a vice presidency at Philadelphia & Reading. Sargent appointed some of those already at Salomon Brothers to his group, and he also hired graduates from the more prestigious business schools.

Salomon Brothers' ongoing relationship with clients in several key industries such as telecommunications, financial services, and utilities helped in the development of its banking business. All of these industries are directly concerned with and influenced by interest rates, so Henry Kaufman's presence was important in winning them over. Nevertheless, in the end the firm's famed placement and pricing abilities proved crucial. Given this power, Salomon often was able to obtain better terms for clients than were available elsewhere.

For example, in 1977, the firm took to market a $60 million Enserch issue with the same coupon with which another underwriter was offering a higher-rated Northern Indiana Public Service issue. In this instance the Salomon Brothers client paid a lower interest rate than otherwise would have been the case. Others took notice. "Salomon went out and aggressively marketed our bonds," said Enserch vice president and treasurer Benjamin Brown. "Their pre-sale indications were very good." Blair Pascoe of Transamerica, another Salomon client won over during this period, echoed the thought. "They are willing to take market risks that others are not willing or able to take."[8] These events marked an acceleration of activities in corporate finance.

"In 1977 we set our sights on expanding market share. We had four clients on the *Fortune* 500; we couldn't tolerate this," said Terry Connelly, one of the young people hired in that period. "We said okay, we'll drive the truck into the *Fortune* 500, and we got tremendous support from the firm." Of the 30 major corporations that changed underwriters in 1978-1980, 12 went to Salomon Brothers largely because of a combination of aggressive salesmanship, ability to place securities, liquidity and market making. In a relatively short time the Salomon Brothers roster of corporate clients included such firms as International Business Machines, International Paper, and American Can. By 1983 Salomon Brothers had done business with 88 of the top 500 companies.[9]

To expand the mergers and acquisitions operations, the firm was once again obliged to seek its principal executive from the outside. J. Ira Harris was emerging as one of the financial district's most respected deal makers. A big man in every way — well over six feet tall and 350 pounds — he was a 31-year-old native New Yorker who came to the Street in the mid-1960s, found employment at Blair & Co., and within two years had shaken up and reformed its merger and acquisitions operation. Harris was a colorful, flamboyant individual, who had a knack of winning the confidence of clients, and who managed often ingenious arrangements to make mergers possible. In 1969 he was recruited by Salomon Brothers to develop these activities from the Chicago office.

When Harris arrived in Chicago he inherited two of Salomon Brothers' more important clients, Esmark and IC Industries, the latter a conglomerate which CEO William Johnson was fashioning around the Illinois Central Railroad. Aware that Johnson was seeking to expand, and knowing that Pepsi-Cola General Bottlers Inc. was interested in being acquired, Harris brought the two together. Even though Pepsi was being sought by other firms and investment bankers, he was able to bring about the $70 million transaction, in part by stressing the compatibility of the two managements.

Other deals followed and the merger business expanded rapidly. Harris orchestrated the sale of *McCall's* magazine by Norton Simon Inc. to the Pritzker interests by utilizing the friendship of Jay Pritzker and David Mahoney, Norton Simon's CEO, to everyone's advantage. In 1973 Harris assisted Walter E. Heller International in purchasing American National Bank & Trust for $109 million. He smoothed relations with Esmark and introduced Donald Kelly to Robert Renekerd, chief executive of Rapid-American's International Playtex Division. Harris worked out an agreement between these two executives, and then went to Rapid-American's chairman Meshulam Riklis, who agreed to sell Playtex to Esmark for $210 million.

Esmark lacked the required cash, so Harris arranged for payment in preferred stock and subordinated debt as well as a relatively small amount of cash. To achieve this, he drew upon Salomon's expertise in marketing securities. Harris was able to persuade Esmark, Rapid-American and other corporations that Salomon was a leader in a broad range of services, and he thereby developed an all-encompassing investment banking arrangement from an initial merger deal. Many others followed, and in each Harris exhibited a brand of astuteness and timing, along with a personal touch, which won the firm the respect of the small fraternity of deal makers, as well as of corporate America.[10]

Salomon Brothers entered every corporate fund-raising activity, from equities and debt to mergers and acquisitions to leasing and the restructuring of balance sheets. In 1973 Salomon Brothers had eleven corporate clients, tieing for sixteenth position, far behind Goldman, Sachs (91), Lehman Brothers (89), Morgan Stanley (61), and First Boston (57). A decade later, in 1984, it had over 400 sovereign and corporate clients worldwide, among them Manufacturers Hanover Trust, Bank of America, American Express Credit, the Southern Railroad, Union Pacific, and Atchison, Topeka & Santa Fe.

While expanding its domestic investment banking and trading operations, Salomon Brothers monitored financial developments abroad. The firm was no stranger to international finance, having marketed Allied bonds during World

War I and having dealt with Latin American and Asian as well as European paper during the 1920s. Nevertheless, no presence actually had been established overseas. During the late 1960s the Executive Committee decided to make the move to Europe because it was one of the most rapidly growing areas in the world for attractive, profitable investments. The European recovery, which began in the late 1950s, had by the late 1960s created a flourishing economy which nevertheless was still susceptible to events in America.

In 1963 the Kennedy Administration imposed an Interest Equalization Tax on Americans who purchased foreign bonds issued in the United States. The clear purpose of this tax was to make it more difficult for foreigners to borrow funds in the American markets, and to effectively cut back on the growing balance of payments deficit. This focused attention on the Eurodollar market, and increased its importance for investment opportunities.

Rather than pay the tax, a number of American and foreign firms conducted part of their dollar borrowings in Europe, even though the Eurobanks charged a slightly higher rate. Further impetus was given by Lyndon Johnson, who two years later, in the foreign credit restraint program, asked banks to agree to "voluntary ceilings on their loans to foreign entities." These measures encouraged American investors to move funds overseas to take advantage of the higher returns.[11]

The effects of these moves on the large American banks were dramatic. When they saw a significant part of their foreign business decline, they hastened to establish overseas branches to protect their interests. By 1965, 13 American banks had 211 branches outside the United States, holding nearly $9 billion in assets, which was three times the amount it had been in 1961.

London, which almost half a century earlier had given way to New York as the world's premier capital market, was at the center of this new flow of money. The major banks there, which had appeared moribund in the immediate post-World War II period, rose to the challenge. No other city, not even New York, had the experience in international finance which had been accumulated by the banks which surrounded the London Stock Exchange and the Bank of England. "They've

London became increasingly important as the Eurodollar market grew. Salomon Brothers established its London affiliate in 1971, and in 1976 Charles McVeigh (standing in rear by window) was named its head.

got everything but the money," said one American banker when describing the London Establishment, "and every banker knows that money comes to people who know how to handle it."[12]

The renewed investment activity originating in London came at the expense of Wall Street. In 1963, approximately 72 percent of all international bonds had been floated in New York; by 1964 the amount had fallen to 55 percent. In that year First National City Bank responded to the challenge by pioneering in the creation of the "Euro-certificate of deposit," which added a new wrinkle to the market. Others followed, as London continued to take the play away from New York. By 1968, the American share of international underwritings had fallen to 28 percent.[13]

These developments demanded creative action from Salomon Brothers, but initially the firm moved with uncharacteristic slowness, caused by the diversion of the rapidly developing domestic market. Discussions regarding a possible international department did not begin in New York until 1968. As had become the rule with such things, it started with a perception of business opportunities and a means whereby clients could be served. A study was made of possible locations, and after surveying the Continent, it was concluded that there were three: some thought Brussels, which was rapidly becoming a focus for European integration; others favored a Swiss locale, since that country was one of the best

International Operations of American Banks, 1964-1973

CATEGORY	1964	1970	1973
U.S. Offices			
Bank credit to foreigners ($billions)	$9.4	$9.7	$17.2
Overseas Branches of U.S. Banks			
Number of banks with overseas branches	11	79	125
Number of overseas branches	181	536	699
Assets of overseas branches ($billions)	$6.9	$52.6	$104.0

Source: Andrew Brimmer and F.R. Dahl, "Growth of American International Banking: Implications for Public Policy," *Journal of Finance*, May, 1975, p. 350.

Estimated Size of the Eurocurrency Market, 1964-1973

(in billions of dollars, end of period)

YEAR	GROSS	NET
1964	12	9
1965	14	12
1966	18	15
1967	23	18
1968	34	25
1969	57	44
1970	75	57
1971	98	71
1972	132	92
1973	191	132

Source: Bank for International Settlements statistics, as cited in Dufey and Giddy, *The International Money Market* (Englewood Cliffs, N.J.: Prentice-Hall, 1978), p. 22.

markets for foreign securities; but London appeared even more attractive. Furthermore, Salomon Brothers as always preferred to train its own people, and switching personnel from the United States to London would not entail a language problem.[14]

The move into Europe took place in 1971. A small office — really a single room with one large desk, a typewriter, and a telex — was rented at One Moorgate, not far from the Bank of England and the London Stock Exchange. The initial contingent of Salomon Brothers International (as the affiliate was to be known) arrived in London on December 14, 1971. The group was headed by a partner, Edgar Aronson, who after serving in the Marines had worked at First National Bank of Chicago in the international area, then moved to Republic Bank and finally went to Salomon Brothers. A serious, intense Harvard graduate, Aronson had more international experience than anyone at the firm outside of Schmeelk's Canadian desk, and had scouted the scene for several months prior to the move.

Moving to England with Aronson were Richard Smith and Randal Etheridge, who were also salesmen, and a British secretary, Tessa Oxtoby. Richard Grand-Jean arrived soon after to explore the possibilities in corporate finance, though little was expected at that time. There was a resemblance to the situation in 1910 at 80 Broadway, when Arthur, Percy, Herbert, and Ben Levy first began the firm. On both occasions the expectations were guarded and carefully thought out. Tessa Oxtoby recalls that one of Aronson's first remarks to her was, "We would like to keep it small."[15]

The original motive was to sell American securities to British and continental institutions, and thereafter expand the client base and get into trading as well. Eventually, Gutfreund and Grand-Jean hoped to underwrite government loans. After this, they planned to expand into the corporate sector and perform a wide variety of investment banking services for European firms.[16]

There was little activity in the first two years, though the firm did take larger quarters at One Moorgate and additional personnel were assigned to London. Then, in a period of less than one year, three developments occurred which altered the market, and with it Salomon Brothers' role overseas.

The first was OPEC's quadrupling of the oil price in late 1973. Saudi Arabia and Kuwait alone earned more than $37 billion in 1974, and more in subsequent years. OPEC insisted payments be made in dollars, which simultaneously enhanced the central role played by that currency and placed pressures upon it. OPEC's most important customers were the Western European nations and Japan, which were left with four options. They could cut down on oil consumption, tax energy heavily to raise the funds with which to pay for imports, increase exports to earn additional revenues, or simply borrow. All were tried, with the last becoming the most important.

Great Britain started the borrowing in March 1974, with a record $2.5 billion Eurocredit flotation. In the next five years Britain, Italy, France, and Spain covered nearly 60 percent of their external financing requirements, approximately $77 billion, through borrowing in the international marketplaces, mostly in London. This obviously created a bonanza for firms prepared to handle underwritings.[17]

The need on the part of the OPEC nations to invest their new wealth was equally important and complementary. Some of the money went into baubles, land, gold, and the like, but most was used to purchase securities. Knowing this, international banks hired experts on the Arab world to travel to the Middle East and solicit business. They were not disappointed; in 1974, OPEC placed $28 billion in the Eurodollar and other markets tied to the dollar, plus $168 billion during the rest of the decade.[18]

Disposition of Oil-Exporting Countries' Identified Cash Surplus, 1974-1980

(in billions of dollars)

YEAR	IDENTIFIED CASH SURPLUS	DISPOSITION	
		Bank Deposits	Other
1974	58	30	28
1975	38	11	27
1976	42	14	28
1977	41	13	28
1978	23	5	18
1979	61	40	21
1980	87	41	46

Source: International Monetary Fund and Bank of England, as cited in R.B. Johnson, *The Economics of the Euro-Market* (New York: St. Martin's, 1982), p. 26.

The second development was directly related to the first. The demand for dollars dictated repeal of the Interest Equalization Tax in January 1974. This opened the New York market once again to foreign borrowers, which some observers expected would cripple the Eurodollar market. Such did not occur. Rather, American firms continued to use that arena to obtain funds for their overseas subsidiaries, preferring London to New York for a variety of reasons, not the least of which being the fact that in New York issues must be registered in the owner's name. What the 1974 repeal meant to foreign investors was that they could purchase American securities more easily, and this too redounded to the benefit of overseas investment firms with knowledge of and experience in the American markets.

This rapidly expanding market was crippled by a bank failure, an indication of just how difficult markets would be in the future. Several officials at the Cologne-based I. D. Herstatt Bank had been speculating unsuccessfully in foreign exchange, and by early summer the bank was illiquid. On June 26, the Bundesbank closed it down, causing consternation throughout the banking world. Other banks also reported losses on foreign exchange transactions — Lloyd's Bank in Lugano lost some $56 million and the Bank of Belgium and the Westdeutsche Landesbank lost more than $100 million each. Now, talk of an international crisis was heard. As it turned out nothing of the sort happened. But other failures of a similar nature took place, among them that of the Franklin National Bank in New York, while the shaky capital markets contributed to other calamities, including the insolvency of New York City itself.[19]

These troubling events deeply affected Salomon Brothers' outlook and its overseas prospects. The Herstatt affair practically closed the international markets for months, and interest rate differentials between the Euro- and U.S. markets widened sharply. Combined with dollar recycling problems and the deepening world recession, this caused grave fears for the stability of the international banking system. Calm was not restored until early 1975, and then only after concerted action to assure liquidity was taken by the leading central banks.

It had become evident that a massive shift in world wealth was taking place. Central banks which previously had few foreign assets to manage now found themselves deeply involved in the international markets, where floating currencies and commercial dislocations made the ground tricky and dangerous. Investors around the world felt the need to diversify their currency holdings, so that the opportunities overseas for placements, swaps, trading, and investment banking became greater than at any time since the 1920s.

Salomon Brothers was eager to capitalize on these opportunities. Within a surprisingly short period, the firm was able to achieve in the international market the scope of development that had taken it half a century to accomplish in the domestic area. The differences between Salomon Brothers and Salomon Brothers International were striking. In the United States the firm was erecting an investment banking business on top of highly developed sales and trading operations. The firm had become famous for its willingness to make secondary markets in all securities it brought out in the primary one. By contrast, in Europe Aronson and Grand-Jean had started out to create a modest sales program and by 1975 had discovered, somewhat to their surprise, that a large trading and investment banking business had followed almost automatically.

Salomon Brothers International planned for growth in its underwriting business in 1975 and 1976. It was hoped that executions in secondary markets would help it develop placement power, and Grand-Jean found that he had stumbled onto virtually virgin territory. Investors were so delighted to have someone to service them in the secondary market that the primary orders followed as a matter of course. In April, 1976, four months after opening a trading operation in these securities, Salomon Brothers International started to manage or co-manage new offerings, and for the next year did them at the rate of more than one a week.[20]

Salomon Brothers International emerged as a worldwide financial power, and this next dictated a move into the Far East. As had been the case with Europe, the firm considered several locales before settling on Hong Kong, which had as many advantages for that part of the world as London did for Europe. Hong Kong was geographically central, it presented no language problem (English being spoken by virtually everyone in the business community), the regulatory and banking environment was patterned after that in the United Kingdom, and communications with the rest of the Pacific Basin were excellent.

To head the pilot operation, Salomon Brothers selected George Hutchinson. He joined the firm in 1970 after having graduated from the University of Washington, spending three years in the Marines, earning an MBA at Columbia University and then working for three years at Smith Barney. After two years in New York he was transferred to London (Aronson tended to favor ex-Marines) in 1972, where he worked in sales. Hutchinson arrived in Hong Kong with two other salesmen — Michael Bowen and John Harada — in August 1976, with a mandate to explore business opportunities throughout Asia. Business was slow at first, but picked up dramatically after the second oil shock. Then Hutchinson and others on his staff started doing a significant business with Pacific Basin governments.

By the late 1970s, it appeared that although Hong Kong offered advantages, there were problems associated with the location, and a move to Tokyo was contemplated. Hong Kong lacked a highly developed and world-scale infrastructure; there were no major insurance companies and only a handful of headquarters banks. Then, too, Asian portfolio management personnel were elsewhere, many in Tokyo. In essence, Hong Kong was small when compared with the giant financial market located in Japan. Thus, Hutchinson suggested that Salomon Brothers International move to Japan and be closer to those who promised to be its major Asian customers.

Salomon Brothers Asia Limited moved to its new headquarters in Tokyo, not far from the Imperial Palace, in 1980. "We sat together on that first day, looked at one another, and began to wonder," recalled Peter Clarke, a salesman who made the switch from Hong Kong. "It was very gloomy. But within three months we had taken on a Japanese salesman, and matters improved. We didn't really get going for six months."[21]

The move proved to be a wise one, for Salomon Brothers pioneered in developing the Japanese market for American securities of all kinds. In fact, local securities firms often purchased American paper for their clients from Salomon Brothers. Moreover, the firm was able to transform the Japanese approach to securities. The Japanese had traditionally tended to purchase stocks and bonds for their portfolios and leave them unmoved, while Salomon was adept at swaps, which were designed to maximize yield and minimize risk. There

The Tokyo Stock Exchange plays a key role in world financial markets. In 1980 the firm established an office in Tokyo for Salomon Brothers Asia Limited.

was another factor, rarely mentioned in American analyses of the Japanese market. According to Hutchinson, "The Japanese insurance companies — a prime market for securities — are very concerned about the great earthquake which is widely expected to occur sometime in the near future. They recognize that if they invest exclusively in Japanese securities they will have a real problem when the time comes to pay claims." This was an aspect of the Japanese securities outlook which Percy Salomon had recognized prior to World War I.

Despite the rapid acceptance of American securities by the Japanese, Asian operations remained more a hope than a reality for the first few years. By 1984, however, the potential of the market started to be realized, especially with the issuance of Euroyen securities in that year. By 1985, Salomon Brothers had professionals at work in Tokyo, covering a region several times greater in size than Europe.

The firm has performed well in placements of securities in Japan, and in dealing with sovereign entities. The challenge that remains is in the area of corporate finance where Japanese and other Asian companies continue to maintain close relationships with their traditional banks.[22]

In the international markets, Salomon Brothers' strength was further enhanced by the arrival in 1977 of James Wolfensohn, the former Executive Deputy Chairman of Schroders Ltd., London, who came to the firm as head of the Corporate Finance Department. An Australian with a Harvard MBA, the 44-year-old Wolfensohn had developed substantial international connections, and while his primary task was to restructure domestic operations, from the outset he also played a role in the international sphere. Wolfensohn had a deep interest in the arts, especially music, and this was more important in European circles than in those on Wall Street.

Thus, as the 1970s drew to a close, Salomon Brothers' positive reputation in international finance was growing apace. "Salomon is clearly the American firm that has come up the fastest in the last two years," said a rival American banker in 1977. "Everyone here talks a good game, but Salomon has gone out and done it." "If a borrower asks me which American investment bank I would recommend for our management group," remarked a European financier, "two times out of three

I would say Salomon Brothers." And another added, "Any firm that wants to be a major factor in investment banking here will have to take a few pages out of the Salomon book."[23]

Throughout, it was John Gutfreund who played the leading role in directing the overseas operations. "John is absolutely the most important guy in our international operation," said Edgar Aronson. Most would agree that he had placed his reputation on the line in this area. Gutfreund persisted, often having to overcome questioning as to the wisdom of the move in the Executive Committee. "My partners don't always agree with me about my world vision," he remarked. "Everybody says, 'The United States is the richest country in the world, so why are you diluting our effort by going around the world?'" The answer is that there was substantial promise in the overseas markets, and in the 1970s, as a half century earlier, Salomon Brothers was constantly seeking new markets and outlets for its energies. Late in the decade it had become obvious that the firm had succeeded there, and that in doing so John Gutfreund had become Bill Salomon's heir apparent.[24]

Chapter VIII

The Turbulent Decade 1969-1978

By the late 1960s, computers, interconnected by telecommunications, were altering the fabric of American life. Nowhere was this more evident than in the financial markets, and the most visible symbol of this modernization was to be found at the New York Stock Exchange. The changes technology brought also fostered a political response in the form of deregulation, which was one of the most significant movements in the post-World War II period. Both deregulation and advanced telecommunications greatly affected Salomon Brothers.

Earlier versions of telecommunications — the telegraph and then the telephone — had enabled the NYSE to become the nation's paramount market in the 19th century. Regional exchanges became all but obsolete as Wall Street was brought within a wire or a call from any part of the nation. The rapid development of wireless in the first quarter of the 20th century did the same for much of the rest of the world, a development which students of business history have termed "the technological imperative."

The impact of new techniques and equipment nibbled away at the foundations of the old market structure in the late 1960s, and altered it completely in the 1970s. In the process, securities firms such as Salomon Brothers had to safeguard their traditional markets and clients, while moving swiftly to develop new areas of investment.

The years from 1969 to 1978 were immensely active ones for the securities industry, especially on the equities side. While there had been much talk of automation in the 1950s, nothing of consequence had really been done about it at the NYSE. However, some over-the-counter dealers had moved aggressively in the new environment. First they challenged the NYSE for block business by utilizing an old technology — the telephone. Then, in the early 1960s, some members experimented with computers and related equipment, seeking to relay information and make trades electronically. They were quite successful. A new term was cropping up on the financial pages to describe what the OTC dealers were creating: "The Third Market," which was dedicated to trading NYSE-listed securities over the counter.

Several other attempts were being made to automate aspects of conducting business, starting with block trading. The NYSE responded by developing its own version of automation called the Block Automation System (BAS) and warned member firms, of which Salomon Brothers was one, against joining AutEx, a private computerized trading information system. Nonetheless, within a year AutEx had 140 subscribers, more than half of which were institutions, and thirty were NYSE members. Thus was born "The Fourth Market."

Such OTC firms as Weeden & Co. and Schapiro & Co. were contesting the legality of NYSE Rule 394, which obliged member firms to deal in listed shares only on the floor. They charged that it prevented them from obtaining the best prices for their customers.

Third Market Volume in NYSE-Listed Stocks, 1965-1972

(in thousands of shares)

YEAR	THIRD MARKET	NYSE	PERCENT
1965	48,361	1,809,350	2.7
1966	58,198	2,204,761	2.6
1967	85,081	2,885,748	2.9
1968	119,730	3,298,664	3.6
1969	155,437	3,173,565	4.9
1970	210,067	3,213,069	6.5
1971	297,850	4,265,279	7.0
1972	327,031	4,496,187	7.3

Source: *The New York Stock Exchange 1973 Fact Book*, p. 15.

Bill Salomon (right) and a bond trader in front of a quote board, soon to be replaced by the displays of sophisticated computers interconnected by telecommunications systems.

In 1971 the National Association of Securities Dealers unveiled its new weapon, the National Association of Securities Dealers Automated Quotation System (NASDAQ). Through the use of electronic consoles, whose essentials could be mastered in a matter of hours by an OTC trader, it was possible for transactions to be made rapidly and at low costs. In 1972 the NASD reported transactions of 327 million listed shares, or well over 7 percent of the business done by the NYSE's specialists.

The emergence of NASDAQ had important implications for Salomon Brothers and other block houses. Block trading had become a good business largely because of fixed commissions. As noted, buyers and sellers of, say, 5,000 shares of a listed stock would pay a commission 50 times that of a 100-share trade, although the transaction's costs were not nearly that much more expensive. In 1969 NYSE Chairman Gustave Levy, who also headed Goldman, Sachs, had told a congressional committee that fixed commissions were at the very heart of the financial system, and that to abandon them would create chaos; he urged legislation to preserve them.

Two years later, however, Levy felt differently. "We'll go along with negotiated rates," he said. "We're flexible." Merrill Lynch Chairman Donald Regan agreed, and he remarked that "fixed commissions are one of the causes of trades leaving the NYSE and going to the Third Market." Regan urged the Exchange to abandon Rule 394 and accept fully negotiated commissions. "There is no assurance that all else will fall into place if it does come; but it is certain that nothing will fall into place without it."[1]

The NYSE was obliged to capitulate to political pressures triggered by the technological imperative. In early 1971, the Securities and Exchange Commission ruled that negotiated commissions on trades of over $500,000 would begin in April 1971, and that the figure would be lowered in stages, with the limit to be reduced to $300,000 one year later. Thus, the large blocks would be the first to feel the impact of deregulation. The thought was that not too soon thereafter all commissions would be negotiated, and this was indeed the case. Just four years later, on May 1, 1975 (a date that will be forever remembered as "May Day" in Wall Street's register) fully negotiated commissions became a fact, and Wall Street was moving toward the development of a central market system, which Bill Salomon thought "could well be the most significant change on our industry's horizon."

The major block houses came to terms with the new technologies. In March 1971, just days prior to the first move to deregulation, the district was in a state of worried anticipation. Knowledgeable observers assumed that Salomon Brothers and Goldman, Sachs would lead the way, setting the tone that others would follow. They concluded that rate-slashing would become epidemic as dealers struggled to retain old clients and win new ones.

Bill Salomon, then a governor of the NYSE, rejected the notion that rates would go so low that others would not be able to compete. A supporter of the Exchange's reform leader, President Robert Haack, Salomon had earlier said that "many of his [Haack's] suggestions would be good for the Street." This earned him the enmity of the Old Guard, yet Salomon persisted, contending that the kinds of institutions that used the services of Salomon Brothers and other block houses were willing to pay for research and also appreciated swift and efficient executions.

He further believed that negotiated commissions were a beneficial force in the industry, because they made possible better services and lower costs to clients. Competition would bring the well-run operations to the forefront, he reasoned. "Why allow the firms that are unsuccessful to dominate any Exchange?" he asked.[2]

April 5, 1972, was the first trading day under the new dispensation for negotiated commissions, and the block houses slugged it out to be first on line. Goldman, Sachs won by a hair; at 10:01 it traded a $4 million, 207,000-share block of Uniroyal, with Salomon Brothers one of the firms close behind. Trading that day was a hectic 17 million shares. Jay Perry remarked, "I've just never seen such chaos down here." Gus Levy said, "We're flexible," and Shields & Co. alluded to John Kennedy: "Let us never negotiate out of fear, but let us never fear to negotiate." John Loeb of Loeb Rhoades tried to hold out, blasting "unrestrained and unrestricted competition." However, two weeks later he took out an advertisement in *The Wall Street Journal* proclaiming, "LOEB RHOADES IS NEGOTIATING." By then the prediction that Salomon Brothers would set the tone had come true. The firm had cut commissions by around 50 percent, and the others followed.[3]

The old Establishment was fading rapidly. Houses such as Salomon Brothers, Merrill Lynch, Goldman, Sachs, and Bear, Stearns were coming to the fore, prompting apocalyptic thoughts that were expressed in 1976 after the trends became clear. "The only Wall Street firms likely to survive outside competition...are the market-makers and dealers such as Goldman, Sachs and Salomon Brothers, the more skilled investment banking firms such as Morgan Stanley, solidly entrenched regional firms such as Dain Kalman & Quail, and a very few of the most efficiently run and imaginative retail firms such as Merrill Lynch and E.F. Hutton. The rest of Wall Street will be slowly swept away."[4]

The block business was still strong, but less lucrative than it had been prior to rate deregulation. There were more players in the field, yet Salomon Brothers remained a leader though the competition was increasing. Block trading in a bull market was far simpler than during bear and ragged markets. By definition the trader was betting against the market, taking on what the seller wanted to dispose of or the buyer hoped

NYSE Large Block Transactions, 1965-1972

YEAR	NUMBER OF TRANSACTIONS	AVERAGE PER SESSION	SHARES (thousands)	PERCENT OF VOLUME
1965	2,171	9	48,262	3.1
1966	3,642	14	85,298	4.5
1967	6,685	27	169,365	6.7
1968	11,254	50	292,680	10.0
1969	15,132	61	402,063	14.1
1970	17,217	68	450,908	15.4
1971	26,941	106	692,536	17.8
1972	31,207	124	766,406	18.5

Source: *The New York Stock Exchange 1973 Fact Book*, p. 73.

to accumulate. This was going on in a market where the institutions increasingly ran in packs.[5]

Salomon Brothers found itself selling to a customer in rallies and buying from it when the market was declining. "Everybody jumps into the same stocks at the same time," noted Salomon's Stanley Shopkorn, who led the way in developing hedging techniques. Often a block positioner would discover he could make a sale only by tying it to a swap. This was a transaction whereby a client would insist on Salomon's buying another security enabling the client to pay in part or in full for the block of stock he was buying from Salomon. For example, on October 25, 1972, the firm executed 17 block trades ranging in size from 32,000 to 360,000 shares, involving almost 3 million shares, on three securities exchanges, and most of these involved swaps. Some took four or five transactions to complete. Swaps often took place in declining markets.[6]

Salomon Brothers also maneuvered to expand its activities in equities research. Until 1974, the firm put out industry reviews without recommendations, which were of relatively little value to those clients who demanded specific recommendations. The firm decided to augment the research department, and its enhanced capabilities, including specific recommendations, provided greater value to the published reports it issued.

The firm moved to increase its commission business so as to justify the increased costs resulting from its enlarged research effort. "What we were trying to do was develop research products which were salable — products which gave customers reasons to do business with us," was the way Shopkorn described what was happening. In the equity business Salomon Brothers was evolving from a trading firm run by traders into what one equities manager called "a trading firm/value added/services firm run by trader-salesmen."[7]

The equities side of the business did not develop to the extent anticipated prior to deregulation and the market collapse. As Gutfreund later remarked, "We overstayed our welcome in the block stock business."[8] Bill Salomon characterized 1972 as a time "marked by continuing transition and uncertainty for the securities industry."

Nonetheless, in 1972 the firm reported its second best year ever, with gross revenues of $203.5 million and income before partners' taxes of $37 million. But the fourth quarter was sluggish, auguring poorly for 1973, a year in which Salomon Brothers' revenues declined to $154 million and the firm posted its first loss, $6.6 million, since 1956. Part of this was due to inflation, a shrinkage of trading volume, high interest rates, and lower securities prices. Even so, Salomon Brothers' net worth came to more than $173 million, making it the largest privately owned investment bank in the United States. A decade earlier the firm's net worth had been only $22 million.[9]

"In 1975 the United States emerged from the worst business recession and severest liquidity crisis since the 1930s." This was Bill Salomon's view toward the end of that year. Salomon Brothers was involved in one of the most dramatic rescue operations in municipal history, and about to undertake an almost equally important salvage operation at one of the nation's leading automobile insurance firms.

By 1975, interest rates had climbed to unprecedented heights, with three-month Treasury bills averaging 7.8 percent and the prime rate over 10.8 percent. Corporations and governments obliged to go to the capital markets to refinance their debt found themselves paying more for money than ever before. Through it all, Salomon Brothers played a central role, raising funds when others shied away from the market, placing its reputation and finances on the line on several occasions to save a number of institutions and firms from the most dire consequences.

For years New York City had borrowed heavily to finance social programs and municipal wage increases. The city was in serious economic trouble. Tax revenues failed to expand, and during the recession business activity declined while unemployment rose. Debt service charges in 1975 were $600 million more than they had been in the previous year; pension costs had increased $500 million during the past two years. When obliged to meet such payments in the past, the city had resorted to short term borrowings. But by the spring of 1975, a generation of such practices had climaxed with a terrible crisis.

Mayor Abraham Beame discovered that it was virtually impossible to market the city's paper, and that the metropolis was without the cash needed to redeem obligations coming due. On April 14, 1975, when several note issues were to mature, Beame failed to sell a $550 million issue of short term obligations. Without funds or the hope of outside assistance, the city had to turn away those owners of paper who demanded payment. Although Beame and others vociferously denied it, New York had practically declared bankruptcy, the first major municipality to do so since the Great Depression.[10]

In the aftermath of the New York default, careers were shattered and reputations brought into question. Mayor Beame was finished as a political force. Both Standard & Poor's and Moody's had maintained their high ratings to the very end, and without this, hundreds of small and institutional investors might not have purchased the city's paper. Even the credibility of these highly respected rating agencies was shaken. There was talk of chicanery, political deals, and criminal action, and investors wondered whether other cities might not follow New York's path into financial distress.

Soon after, it was evident that the state of Massachusetts also was in serious trouble. Massachusetts would have to borrow some half a billion dollars in order to remain liquid. Understandably, quotations for municipal bonds sank, interest rates soared, and the tax-exempt market was in shambles.

Salomon Brothers played a crucial and interesting role in those frightening moments. A former partner and member of the Executive Committee, William Simon, had emerged as a powerful and contentious spokesman on fiscal matters for the Gerald Ford administration. Simon had left Salomon Brothers in 1972 to become deputy to the Secretary of the Treasury, and the following year was named Director of the Federal Energy Office. In 1974 President Ford selected Simon to become Secretary of the Treasury, and now he was deemed one of the most powerful figures in Washington. Given his position and experience in the municipal bond market, Simon was the obvious candidate to handle the debt crisis when Mayor Beame appealed to Washington and Albany for assistance.

Simon thought that a federal guarantee program "of limited scope and duration" might be established. He stated the case with forceful rhetoric, telling a congressional investigating committee that "the financial terms of assistance [should] be made so punitive, the overall experience be made so painful, that no city, no political subdivision, would ever be tempted to go down the same road."[11]

William E. Simon

Mayor Beame and Governor Hugh Carey attempted to funnel additional state aid to the city. Governor Carey established an advisory panel comprised of Felix Rohatyn and Richard Shinn, the Chairman of Metropolitan Life, and Donald Smiley, the Chairman of Macy's, who were both lawyers. The panel recommended creation of the Municipal Assistance Corporation, which was promptly christened "Big Mac" by the media.

A state agency, MAC was empowered to collect the sales tax and the stock transfer tax in the city, and use this revenue stream to back the issuance of debt instruments. Some MAC bonds were to be used to pay off holders of the city's obligations, while the more prominent banks purchased sufficient bonds to carry New York through the summer. However, bond prices declined in the secondary market, causing consternation at MAC, where Rohatyn realized a public offering was needed to provide the agency with the necessary credibility.

The situation invited comparisons with the 1907 banking panic, when the financial community marshalled forces to rescue the entire American financial structure. While there was no sign of complete collapse in 1975, a pall hung over the tax-exempt sector in late June as the issue was being discussed. Matters became complicated when it was learned that the city's budget deficit for the past two years had been understated. The financial community gathered forces for the rescue operation in this desperate atmosphere.

On June 25, 1975, a syndicate was formed to handle the MAC offerings. It was led by Salomon Brothers (from the investment banking side) and Morgan Guaranty Trust (for the commercial banks), and these two brought in 363 other financial institutions. The initial underwriting was to be $1 billion with maturities running from 1977 to 1990, and interest rates of from 6.5 percent to 9.5 percent, which made it the largest municipal flotation in history. It was publicized as being the first of several issues to be offered that summer, geared to raise a total of $3 billion. Moody's rated the issues at A, while Standard & Poor's gave them an A+ rating, leading Mayor Beame to charge that it is "incredible that MAC, an instrument of New York State, acting on behalf of the city, is forced to sell bonds at an interest rate exceeding 9 percent."

The financial community disagreed. Banks and other institutions took $650 million of the issue, but it was clear that it would be difficult to distribute the rest. To add to the difficulties, the MAC bonds came out on July 1, 1975, only one day after a similar Massachusetts bailout of $450 million. Furthermore, a total of nearly $21 billion in new corporates had been sold in the first half of the year. (For the entire year of 1974, $27 billion had been sold, and at the time that had been a new record.) Finally, some $2.88 billion in long term state and city bonds had been floated in June, also a new record.[12]

The syndicate overcame all these obstacles and sold virtually the entire issue in two days, in a calm fashion. "There was no panic," said John O'Brien, who had just arrived at Salomon Brothers. "It seemed under control. The rest of the market fell precipitously, and losses were taken. But there was hope — there seemed to be hope something would work out." It was later disclosed that the sale might even have been completed in a shorter time were it not for the fact that both Morgan Guaranty and Salomon Brothers were swamped by the paperwork.[13]

The huge underwriting was hailed as a remarkable achievement, and one that not only established MAC as a viable entity, but apparently assured its success in future financings. Perhaps the crisis was not as dramatic as the 1907 operation, but it nevertheless brought forth an impressive display of cooperation and placement power.

There were two interesting sidelights to this gigantic and successful undertaking. In the first place, few were surprised that Salomon Brothers had taken the lead for the investment banks, since the firm was acknowledged to be one of the district's leaders. But what was intriguing was that it was done through cooperation with Morgan Guaranty, historically the apotheosis of the Old Guard. By 1975 Salomon Brothers not only was a member of the new Establishment, but had become one of its most important players.

Salomon Brothers' ability to perform well in difficult circumstances was illustrated once again the following year when it helped restructure Government Employees Insurance Company (GEICO). A 40-year-old firm which started out by insuring low-risk automobile drivers, GEICO had become one of the nation's largest insurers by 1976. In the process the firm had departed from its original approach by entering higher-risk areas in the casualty business and competing fiercely by lowering premium charges. This enabled GEICO to expand rapidly, but also placed it in a precarious financial position. From 1972 to 1975 its underwriting ratio (insurance losses plus costs as a percentage of premiums) shot up from 94 percent to 124 percent.

Like so many other corporate problems in this period, the increase was due in large part to inflation. The costs of auto repairs and claim settlements soared. Meanwhile, the institution of no-fault insurance in several states and the reluctance of regulators to grant major rate increases had caused premium income to rise sluggishly. GEICO was not the only insurance company to feel the pinch, but because of its aggressive pricing its existence was imperiled.

In 1975, GEICO brought in a new Chief Executive Officer, John Byrne, Jr., formerly executive vice president at The Travelers Corp., with a mandate to develop a plan to save the firm from liquidation. First, Byrne instituted "Operation Bootstrap," under which more than 100 offices were closed and the work force was cut from 7,000 to 4,000. Rates were raised, and GEICO left some states where underwritings were unprofitable. To raise capital in order to remain afloat, Byrne hoped to issue new common shares and sell them to his reinsurers, so that in the end they would own 25 percent of the outstanding equity. His hope was that they would agree in order to maintain their business relationships with GEICO. Next, Byrne wanted to sell preferred shares to existing stockholders, in order to establish a financial cushion while restructuring proceeded.

The reinsurers refused to accept this program, stating they would not purchase shares unless Byrne raised the other funds simultaneously. Thus, his two-part plan revolved around a public underwriting of stock. Salomon Brothers entered the picture at this point in the life-or-death struggle of GEICO.

In July 1976, GEICO asked Salomon Brothers' insurance research specialist Michael Frinquelli to set up a meeting between the company and analysts at Salomon Brothers and other firms. Later, Byrne scouted the district to discover what interest existed there for a GEICO underwriting, and found that most rejected the notion. However, John Gutfreund sensed that GEICO could be salvaged, and he was particularly impressed with Byrne's abilities and dedication. Telling Byrne, "We'll take a look at it," Gutfreund had Salomon Brothers prepare a written prospectus, which was reviewed by the SEC after several drafts.

In November 1976, GEICO was clearly in a parlous state. Gutfreund attempted to create a syndicate to market $75 million in GEICO preferred, but could find no takers. In fact, the reinsurers were showing signs of backing down. GEICO common, which four years earlier had sold for 61, was by then under 3 and slipping. Faced with the alternatives of dropping the underwriting altogether or taking the issue to market alone, Gutfreund opted for the latter.

In the days immediately prior to the offering, it appeared that Salomon Brothers had blundered, and that Gutfreund would have to take responsibility for a major loss. But there were some indications of confidence in the firm's action. GEICO common started to rise, because some believed that Salomon Brothers' willingness to underwrite the issue was assurance of its ultimate liquidity.

The underwriting proved a success; the existing stockholders took more shares than expected, and Salomon Brothers had little trouble selling the rest because of its placement power. Byrne was able to turn the company around. Within a year it once again was profitable, and in fact reinstated the payment of cash dividends, while the price of the common more than doubled. "Investors are reacting to good earnings reports," wrote one analyst. "But I don't think they have fully appraised what has happened at the company. It has...the best management I've seen in the industry."

None of this could have been possible, however, without that 1976 underwriting — which in turn, would not have taken place unless John Gutfreund perceived as much at that time. It was one of the many examples when his business insight, combined with his ability to evaluate people in a very human way, brought success to the firm.[14]

This achievement was accomplished in the face of a hostile market environment, which continued into the following year. Nevertheless, Salomon Brothers progressed and expanded. In fiscal 1978 the firm purchased or sold over $500 billion worth of securities, municipal financings came to $10.5 billion, and the firm's net worth rose to $208.7 million, all of these figures being records. While retaining its traditionally close relations with financial institutions, railroads and utilities, Salomon had developed an important following among the nation's major industrial firms as well. By 1978 there were 49 general partners and 1,600 employees at Salomon Brothers, more than doubling the figure of 24 general partners and 746 employees of just a decade earlier.

It was known within the firm and the financial district that Bill Salomon intended to resign as Managing Partner at the close of the 1978 fiscal year, and that he would be succeeded by John Gutfreund. In fact, this had been assumed since 1975. Bill Simon had been the only possible contender for the succession. The contrast between the two men was interesting. Simon was a famed conservative Republican with ambitions for the White House, while Gutfreund had supported George McGovern's presidential bid in 1972, and was an unabashed liberal Democrat.

Simon was brash and outspoken, while Gutfreund had become reflective in his public utterances over the years. More to the point, Gutfreund had devoted his professional life to the firm and was prepared to continue on in the same manner. Had Simon not left and developed outside interests, he might have given Gutfreund a contest for the top position. But even if Simon had returned to Salomon after leaving government service, Gutfreund would have had the edge because of his leadership in so many areas of the firm's activities and his experience with the personnel and principles of the firm. The comparative figures during the time of Gutfreund's growing influence in the direction of the firm tell the story.

The contrast between Bill Salomon and John Gutfreund is striking. By 1977 Bill Salomon had become an elder statesman, one of the most respected individuals in the district, widely credited with having steered Salomon Brothers

Salomon Brothers: Selected Statistics, 1965, 1978 and 1984

(in millions of dollars)

	YEAR		
	1965	1978	1984
Pre-Tax Income	3.7	26.5	557.0
Net Worth	19.7*	150.6	1,383.1
Tax-Exempt Offerings	NA	10,500.2	33,053.5
Corporate Offerings	924.7	13,793.2	35,083.2
Eurobond Offerings	—	1,734.8	41,606.2

* Capital accounts of 6/30/65.
Source: Salomon Brothers, *Annual Reviews*, 1978, 1984; *Investment Dealers' Digest*.

to its position of eminence, while Gutfreund was perceived as a daring and imaginative trader and a person of exceptional vision.

Their managerial styles were quite different. Salomon would give a hearing to everyone involved in a matter under consideration, and then make the decision on his own, with the others expected to follow. In contrast, Gutfreund liked to involve the people who would be affected by a decision while it was being made, and would bend over backward to make them comfortable with what was to be done. Nevertheless, Gutfreund is in ultimate control of the executive function of the firm, and his decisions after consultations are final.

In style, viewpoint, and approach, each was well suited for the period in which he led the firm. Bill Salomon had come to leadership at a time when the district was dominated by the old Establishment and Salomon Brothers was being run by men who had come up the hard way, through the booming 1920s, the Great Depression, and World War II. Under his guidance Salomon Brothers had undergone phenomenal growth.

In Salomon's day the challenge was to take the firm from its position as a well-considered but relatively minor force in bonds, and move it into one where it could compete with the best and most prestigious of the established firms for clients and markets. This he had done with verve and panache, and by 1978, Salomon Brothers was deemed a leader and at the cutting edge in the district. As Gutfreund put it the following year, "For good or bad, we are totally members of the club and have been for some time.... Salomon Brothers as a house did not change the club. We joined it."[15]

Bill Salomon retained earnings which were used to expand operations in conventional markets, and he also helped put together the teams which moved swiftly into new areas. These included activities in competitive bidding, investment banking, research, international operations, mortgage-backed securities, and more. Under his guidance, talented and aggressive individuals such as John Gutfreund, Sidney Homer, Henry Kaufman, Ira Harris, Bill Simon, James Wolfensohn, Edgar Aronson, and others spearheaded the move into these areas, and ultimately became the trailblazers, developing instruments and strategies that other firms would imitate.

By the early 1970s Gutfreund had become first among equals behind Salomon, and the clear heir apparent. When he stepped into the position as managing partner in 1978, Gutfreund brought different talents and insights to a rapidly changing Wall Street scene, and they were equally appropriate for the new era then emerging. His vision was quite broad. He saw the trend toward a common capital market worldwide and perceived what should be done to put the firm in a position to take advantage of it. Along with internationalization, he was acutely aware of the significance of institutional dominance of the marketplace. He could see the key role of innovation and supported pioneering efforts in various fields. Gutfreund also saw the roles technology and communications

John Gutfreund (left) became Managing Partner upon the retirement of William Salomon on September 30, 1978, in a smooth management transition.

were playing in creating change, and he understood how to harness these powerful new tools to the benefit of the firm. These were the dynamics of the new era, and the new chief executive's thinking was keyed to them.

Above all, Gutfreund was aware of the crucial human element. By the 1970s a new breed had arrived on the Street. It included MBAs from prestigious universities, entrepreneurs who had experience in small high-technology companies, men and women who were widely traveled and sophisticated while still in their twenties. They were the ones who would understand the new techniques and generate the new ideas that would mean success or failure.

John Gutfreund recognized that Salomon Brothers was operating on quite a different kind of terrain from the one that had existed when he first joined the firm. In those days traders dealt with their counterparts at other houses, while salesmen worked with portfolio managers at insurance firms and banks. Now, the firm's executives cooperated not only with officers at many of the nation's largest corporations, but also with prime ministers and treasury officials of foreign governments, and governors, mayors, and cabinet members in the United States.

Moreover, the markets were strikingly different, owing to the almost revolutionary alterations in the financial structure which began in the 1970s. In his early years at the helm, Bill Salomon had to elbow his way into the Wall Street Establishment. Near the end of his tenure he gave Gutfreund and others behind him opportunities to take the firm into the national and then international arenas.

All of this meant a tremendous expansion of facilities and personnel. When Bill Salomon became Managing Partner, there were only a handful of traders and salesmen in the firm; by the time he was preparing to step down, Salomon Brothers had over 1,600 employees, of whom more than 500 might be categorized as "decision makers" — far too many to keep in touch with on a day-to-day basis.

One of Gutfreund's most difficult tasks was to retain the virtues of the old free-wheeling operations, in which individuals were encouraged to expand their scope and innovate as much and far as their talents and opportunities permitted. While continuing to encourage this initiative, he succeeded in imposing upon the firm a new structure to better focus all energies. As he described it later on, the idea was to centralize management, to make it "top-led but bottom-driven." In many ways, the challenges he faced were even greater than those posed to Bill Salomon in his day; they were

Salomon Brothers' Executive Committee in 1979 (from left): James D. Wolfensohn, Henry Kaufman, Managing Partner John H. Gutfreund, J. Ira Harris, Richard G. Rosenthal, Vincent B. Murphy, Jr., Gedale B. Horowitz and Richard J. Schmeelk.

much more complex and convoluted because of the increasing sophistication of every aspect of the district and the international financial world.

The transition on September 30, 1978, went smoothly. Bill Salomon became a limited partner and honorary member of the Executive Committee, and Gutfreund assumed command that morning. Gutfreund's greatest immediate concerns were personnel and new business. Salomon Brothers is a firm in which having the right individuals in place has always been and continues to be vital. Gutfreund recognized the need to bring in and train additional personnel to support the firm's tremendous expansion.[16]

As for new business, Salomon was just pioneering a field which Gutfreund later would describe as "larger than the government, stock, corporate, and municipal bond markets combined — all of them in the aggregate aren't as large as the mortgage market."[17]

Chapter IX

Transition and Opportunity 1976-1982

In John Gutfreund's first years as Salomon Brothers' Chief Executive Officer, the firm sought new areas of activity while expanding from its traditional base. "What Salomon has that no other major firm has is a tremendous flexibility to let your skills end up where they are most productive," said Robert Dall, whose career was a good demonstration of this, in the form of his switch from the firm's money market desk to head a venture in mortgage-backed securities.[1]

During this period Gutfreund's managerial concepts were put into daily practice. He sought a firm that, while strongly directed from the top, permitted maximum flexibility and initiatives among individuals. He advanced young people in ground-breaking fields and encouraged justifiable risk taking and financial creativity under the overall guidance of the Executive Committee, which he led.

A prime example was Salomon Brothers' pioneering in the mortgage market. The firm had been monitoring this sector since the early 1970s. Mortgages were an unusual investment opportunity that had been ignored by Wall Street, since they had always been considered the province of savings and loan associations. With almost $700 billion in mortgages outstanding in 1976, that market clearly merited the serious consideration given to it by the people at Salomon Brothers. Based on its careful analysis, the firm committed itself to mortgage-backed securities and, in this, made perhaps its greatest single contribution to the investment industry.

The institutional structure of the mortgage market was changing rapidly during the 1970s. After the courts ruled in 1969 that Federal National Mortgage Association (known as "Fannie Mae") borrowings had to be considered part of the federal deficit, an amendment was made to the Housing Act. At the time, Fannie Mae was the nation's largest mortgage insurer. Its function was to purchase mortgages from the thrifts and sell them to investors interested in high-yielding, insured paper. The gigantic agency was transformed into a publicly owned corporation and given the authority to raise funds on the open market, with an implied mandate to expand operations significantly.

Another agency was also created for this task, the Government National Mortgage Association, not surprisingly known as "Ginnie Mae." It was established by the same Housing Act amendment to take over functions formerly carried out by Fannie Mae. Funded by the federal government and controlled by the Department of Housing and Urban Development, Ginnie Mae purchased Federal Housing Administration and Veterans Administration mortgages, added its own guarantee, and then bundled them together in units to be offered for sale to investors. Ginnie Maes quickly became popular, especially with the more liquid thrifts, which in the early 1970s proved to be their best customers.

In order to provide comparable support for the thrift institutions which made conventional loans, and because Fannie Mae was slow in moving into the field, the Federal Home Loan Bank organized the Federal Home Loan Mortgage Corporation, which was promptly dubbed "Freddie Mac." Like Fannie Mae, it sold bonds and notes on the open market and used the proceeds to purchase conventional mortgages from the thrifts, and thus it complemented the other two agencies.[2]

The initial Ginnie Mae certificates were assembled in December 1970, but only after a policy disagreement was resolved between two forces at the Department of Housing and Urban Development. One wished the security to be structured like a municipal bond, which is to say there would be issues of individual serial bonds with a term bond at the end to match the cash flows of the typical mortgage. An opposing group favored creating securities which resembled the mortgages themselves, and would "pass through" to the owners both principal and interest on a monthly basis.

As the nation's largest and most important dealer in all forms of government paper, Salomon Brothers was consulted on this matter. The key individual for the firm was William Simon. In his customarily forceful manner, Simon argued for the former kind of certificate and against the pass-throughs. One reason was that he believed that investors would not be familiar with the latter system. The proposed pass-throughs would be the only bond-like certificate in which principal was returned regularly rather than at maturity, and he felt this would detract from their appeal.

Moreover, under this proposal, investors would receive varying payments since a certificate owner would receive a lump sum as the mortgages were retired. Furthermore, he argued that in the certificate's early period much of the payment would be interest, little of it principal, but that this would change each month and present tax complications. Yet another consideration was that, unlike most bonds, the holder would have no "call protection." For example,

John Gutfreund (standing far right) continues the tradition of managing the firm from The Room, Salomon Brothers' bi-level sales and trading area. This is the

the owner of a Ginnie Mae might find that when mortgage rates declined many of the mortgages would be refinanced, leaving him out in the cold.

Obviously, Simon was displeased when the government nevertheless decided in favor of the pass-throughs, against his advice. He realized that Salomon Brothers could not ignore so important a new investment medium, but he did not involve the firm very forcefully in Ginnie Maes. Simon selected Ernest Werlin, a relative newcomer from Corporate Finance who had little exposure to bonds, to lead the effort. In this way Salomon Brothers entered the business as a minor player. The field consequently was led by First Boston, F.S. Smithers & Co., Merrill Lynch, Bache, and Loeb Rhoades. Simon refused to hire "originators," individuals who would go to the thrifts, gather mortgages together, package them, and then offer the paper to investors.

integrating focus for syndication, distribution and market-making in government and corporate issues, money market instruments and mortgage-backed securities.

It appeared at the time that the firm would be content with this minor role, and that Salomon Brothers did not consider mortgages very important. Not that it seemed to matter. Relatively few investors really understood the paper, and there was no secondary market for either Ginnie Maes or, later, Freddie Macs, and thus little or no liquidity in them. Understandably, the new instruments were not well received in the district. The situation in the mortgage field in the mid-1970s was characterized by unfamiliarity with the instrument and by market volatility. This was combined with lack of trained personnel and good opportunities elsewhere (especially overseas), so prudence dictated caution.

Moreover, Salomon Brothers underwent an experience which further soured the firm on Ginnie Maes. Two $75 million Ginnie Mae offerings were purchased from a West Coast mortgage banker, one a 6½ percent coupon, the other an 8 percent coupon, after which they were sold. In the process, the operations department mixed up the two issues, registering each to the wrong customers. The certificates were then delivered to Bache on a Friday, where they were broken down into thousands of securities. Because of the error the securities were incorrectly registered by Ginnie Mae and they were undeliverable, which meant Bache would not have to pay for them. Meanwhile, Salomon Brothers was responsible for payment to the mortgage banker. In other words, they had to be paid for but could not be sold. Given the firm's finances at the time, this might have resulted in technical bankruptcy.

Bill Simon put in a rush call to Bache asking for a continuance until Monday morning. Robert Dall, who was in charge of the Money Desk (which financed operations), contacted Ginnie Mae, explained the situation, and asked for permission to fly a squad of Salomon Brothers secretaries to Washington to retype the certificates so they could be delivered to Bache on Monday. Both Bache and Ginnie Mae agreed, and after a hectic weekend the certificates were delivered.

With this incident, Dall entered the mortgage area for Salomon Brothers and became its key man there. He took charge of the Ginnie Mae business for the firm, with a mandate to develop it in the way he thought best.

In 1974, Ginnie Mae was asked by the Treasury to dispose of a large block of mortgages which had been acquired by the government under subsidy programs and below market rates. Gutfreund, Dall and others urged Daniel Kearney, then head of Ginnie Mae, to offer them through all-or-none auctions open to financial houses. This would bring in Wall Street, which would sell them to the investing public, thus giving Ginnie Maes more visibility. The idea was accepted and two syndicates — one led by Salomon Brothers, the other by Merrill Lynch and First Boston on a rotating basis — were put together to bid on 23 consecutive monthly auctions, each of more than $200 million in mortgages. The first auction was a success, and Salomon Brothers began to grow more interested in the product.

By 1975, Ginnie Mae certificates were being sold to a variety of institutional investors. Some $7.4 billion of mortgages were packaged and sold in that year, while the figure for 1976 was $13.5 billion, of which approximately half went to large institutions, especially pension funds, and half were bought by the thrifts.

Freddie Macs were also slow starters originally, with only $1.5 billion of them sold in 1976; but even so, interest in them was growing. That year a total of over $15 billion in mortgage-backed securities established these instruments as important competitors to the older forms of fixed income vehicles. According to financial writer Dana Thomas, "This small group [of firms with experience in the area by 1977], including Salomon Brothers, Merrill Lynch, Loeb Rhoades, First Boston, Blyth Eastman Dillon, and Bache Halsey Stuart, has done 80 percent of the business."[3]

The nation was still in the grip of stagflation during the latter years of the 1970s, when many of the "rules" by which economists had lived for generations seemed to have gone awry. At a time when the economy was generally sluggish and when, according to recognized economic theories, there should have been little or no inflation, prices were rising sharply. Nowhere was this more visible or far-reaching in impact than in housing, where high down payments were required and mortgage rates were in the double digits. A house which ten years earlier might have sold for $20,000, with a down payment of $7,000 and a 6 percent mortgage on the rest, might have been offered at $80,000 with a 15 percent, $40,000 mortgage.

Many thrifts had difficulties meeting the demand for mortgages, since depositors were closing their accounts, and for good reason. Why would an investor accept 5¼ percent interest from a thrift when an uninsured money market fund was offering more than twice that rate, and completely secure Treasury bills were readily available at only a slightly lower yield than the funds?

In 1978 the thrifts received permission to sell short term certificates in order to compete with the money market accounts. While this program pulled in funds, they were at full market rates (of around 9.5 percent that year), which put great pressure on profit margins. A mature S&L of the late 1970s might have a large portfolio of 6 and 7 percent mortgages, while paying close to twice as much for new money.

The Mortgage Securities Department was led in 1981 by Managing Directors (from left) Lewis Ranieri and Robert Dall, pioneers in restructuring the financing of housing.

It was hardly surprising that a large number of them reported deficits. Stated simply, the price of borrowing short and lending long had placed the industry in a vise which squeezed profits mercilessly.

Thus, stagflation had a severe impact on housing, and new starts declined precipitously. In 1978, there were more than 2 million new structures started, but two years later the figure fell to under 1 million for the first time since the end of World War II. It was a dangerous situation for the national economy. A return to prosperity and a higher standard of living would be impossible without a revival in housing, and a collapse of the thrift industry would result in a general financial panic. The thrifts were in dire circumstances due to astronomical mortgage rates, illiquidity, disintermediation, and the continuing need to borrow short and lend long in a high interest rate environment.

Salomon Brothers helped change this situation. Dall noted that FHA and VA mortgages constituted only 15 percent of the total outstanding. The rest were being insured by private agencies, and so he sought to create what amounted to private pass-throughs. Working with the Bank of America, Salomon Brothers developed such certificates, and in late 1977 brought the first Bank of America issue to market.[4]

At this time Gutfreund asked Dall to draw up a proposal regarding Salomon Brothers' future in the field. Dall recommended the creation of a wholly integrated department which would embrace research, sales and trading, and would be separate from the Government Bond Department. The report was accepted and the Mortgage Securities Department was created. Dall was placed in charge and he obtained the services of Lewis Ranieri as senior trader.[5]

Then 30 years old, Ranieri was once described by a financial writer as looking and acting like "an honest kid from Brooklyn." A competitor said that "he's the kind of enthusiastic proselytizer who was born to work on new frontiers." Robert Schiffer, who, as President of Huntoon Paige and Company, did massive joint ventures with Salomon Brothers, added, "You have to hand it to him: he's a business genius." Dall recognized these talents from the first, and this was the main reason he wanted Ranieri with him.[6]

Ranieri had arrived at the firm in an unusual fashion. As a boy, he had expected to follow an uncle into the restaurant business, but allergies eventually prevented him, and in 1967, he entered St. John's University to major in English literature. Seeking a night job to pay his way, he obtained a job as a $70-a-week mail clerk at Salomon Brothers. He remembers that his future at the firm seemed very uncertain at the time.

Three months after he started the job, Ranieri's wife fell ill and had to be hospitalized. His medical bills mounted to more than $10,000. He was desperate, and asked his supervisor whether an advance on his salary could possibly be arranged, half expecting to be fired. Instead, Ranieri was told to come around in the morning to speak about it with the person in charge of the section. He did so and was informed, "It's taken care of." Thinking this meant the amount would be deducted from his paycheck indefinitely, Ranieri started to protest, but was interrupted by a soft, "I told you; it's been taken care of." He was not expected to return the money. "I was just a clerk, there a few months," said Ranieri, "but they knew I was in a jam and they helped me out. That's the way Salomon is. No other firm on the Street takes care of its people that way."[7]

Ranieri won promotions in the operations end of the firm, and seven years later Vincent Murphy gave him the primary responsibility for setting up the computer system. He knew, however, that the real action was in trading and sales. "One of my personal drawbacks is that I become bored quickly," he once remarked. "I've done a lot of things, from cab driving to short order cook. You name it, I've done it."

In 1974 Ranieri was offered the opportunity to become a trader, so he took a cut in salary and status and went to the floor as a clerk. "It was a risk," Ranieri conceded, but one he deemed worth taking. "At Salomon Brothers trading is the heart of the business. Lots of the partners have come out of there."[8]

Ranieri clearly had a knack for the work of a trader. Within less than a year, he had a spot in the utility bond area and was a senior trader, when he was called in by Dall to assume a similar position in mortgage-backed securities. "They weren't enthusiastic," he recalled, "because it was a risk for them to take one of their senior traders and put him in an area that no one even knew existed, let alone understood."[9]

Dall and Ranieri began with a small staff, but they had an audacious and ambitious plan. They estimated that the thrifts would never again be able to take as commanding a position in the mortgage market as they had prior to the late 1970s. A vacuum had been created that could be filled by the capital markets, and it could be done by securitizing mortgages in a variety of forms.

Their idea was nothing less than to restructure the entire housing market rather than merely creating securities. This involved realigning the largest industry in the country, and made it Salomon Brothers' most ambitious undertaking to date. Clients would have to be educated in all aspects of the new securities, and shown the potential of the business for profitable investment. "All the other markets we know — the capital markets, governments, municipals, equities — grew up over time with a support web of regulations and trading norms, legal status, etc." noted Ranieri. "They grew slowly over many generations. But there was no mortgage market until this generation."[10]

The Mortgage Securities Department got off to a slow start because of the depressed market and the sheer originality of the idea. Dall and Ranieri shuttled back and forth between New York and Washington, arranging deals for FHA projects, for conventional pass-throughs, and for private placements, which enabled the firm to earn approximately $6 million in the first year and, more important, prepared it for the revival in housing that occurred in 1982. Their aggressive salesmanship in the market for mortgage-backed securities invigorated the housing market itself, and when that happened, said Laurence Fink of rival First Boston, "Salomon was in the driver's seat. They had the commitment, the bodies, and the investment banking ties with thrifts."[11]

The experience with mortgages indicated that the many faces of banking were changing rapidly. "A few years ago you could describe the banking industry as a group of institutions with defined characteristics," one banker recently told author Martin Mayer. "In the 1990s you'll have to describe it as a group of services provided by a range of institutions." "We're trying to make a decision about what a bank is," said Federal Reserve Board Chairman Paul Volcker. "My instinct is that there's something unique about a bank." But he was not quite certain what that might be.[12]

Volcker's puzzlement was understandable. American Express owned commercial banks and a brokerage firm. Sears Roebuck had both and a major real estate operation as well. Chase Manhattan Bank and the Bank of America ran discount brokerages, and the strictures forbidding commercial banks from conducting investment banking functions were being skirted. Merrill Lynch was transforming itself into a veritable financial supermarket, and all lines of financial enterprise were becoming blurred.

While observers of the district wondered which investment house would be the next to merge into some other giant firm and in what form, few considered Salomon Brothers as likely to seek this route of expansion. Other investment banks, including Lehman Brothers, Lazard Frères, First Boston, and even Goldman, Sachs were deemed possible candidates; Salomon Brothers was not included, for obvious and convincing reasons.

In the first place, Salomon Brothers' capital resources at the end of fiscal 1980 came to more than $330 million, which made it the strongest privately owned investment banking and market-making firm in the United States. In size it was second only to the publicly owned Merrill Lynch within the industry. Moreover, the firm's unique style and strong image appeared to militate against a merger with any other entity, a move that could dilute or alter its position negatively. Bill Salomon had strongly opposed a merger of any kind, and most knowledgeable people thought that John Gutfreund was of a like mind.

However, mergers of investment banks were occurring with increasing frequency, and many of the oldest names on the Street either came together or disappeared into the maw of one financial conglomerate or another. In 1978, Lehman Brothers and Kuhn, Loeb joined forces, and Dean Witter merged with Reynolds Securities to form Dean Witter

Reynolds. This was a prelude to its later buyout by Sears Roebuck. In 1979, the recently created Shearson Hayden Stone united with another relatively newly merged institution, Loeb Rhoades Hornblower. From this merger came Shearson Loeb Rhoades, which later was acquired by American Express. That same year, Paine Webber bought out Blyth Eastman Dillon for $45 million. In 1981 Prudential purchased Bache Halsey Stuart for $385 million, followed by the American Express purchase of Shearson for $864 million.[13]

In this superheated atmosphere, there was much hopping about from firm to firm as the Wall Street houses bid frantically against one another for experts in the new investment areas. People were always the key. J. Steven Manolis, on his way to a Salomon Brothers partnership at the age of 26 because of his early success in the corporate bond field, offered the most plausible reason. "The great thing about this business is that you can become an expert in a very short time," he said. "The reason is that it is so fresh and always changing. Our business is capricious and dynamic. In six months you can know more than anyone else in mortgage bonds."[14]

The personnel factor was most evident in the mortgage-backed securities area. Salomon Brothers and First Boston had organized their desks before the others and were prime targets for raiders. "Now they are serving as a pool of talent for others trying to get into the business," said Stephen Joseph, who was in a position to know, having gone from Salomon Brothers to Drexel Burnham Lambert.[15]

Movement among staff has always taken place during flush periods on the Street. Traders and salesmen hasten to grab the golden ring when the opportunity presents itself to them. A bright young person whose record is above average expects a partnership within six or seven years of arrival, and the failure to win this promotion is regarded as a sign that the time has come to move on.

Attaining a partnership at Salomon Brothers was deemed to be one of the most certain paths to financial success. One client put it this way: "Being a partner in that firm is the closest thing to being a partner in the U.S. Treasury."

But in 1981 there was a movement which indicated that a fierce competitiveness had developed that might well have eroded the Salomon *élan*.[16]

Salomon had some personnel problems, one of which was generational. By 1981, the last of the founding group had been replaced by the new breed out of the MBA programs and law schools. Tom Strauss, a University of Pennsylvania graduate who was a managing director in government bonds and a member of the Executive Committee, noted the tensions which had existed between these two groups in the 1960s and 1970s. "There was some resentment," he observed. "You had to work at it. But you were aware that they were aware that there was a difference. They saw the new people coming into the firm and, in essence, move right by them. So there was a cultural and educational gap. There were some difficult moments, because we were in the process of a transition [from a firm which was much smaller and less sophisticated] to one with much higher educational standards, where the firm was going to be managed by a much different kind of person."[17]

By the very fact that it was one of the great training grounds for the industry, Salomon Brothers' people were often sought by other firms. The senior people devoted a great deal of their time to retention of valued individuals. It was reflected in their talks to trainees. "One course they should stress at the graduate schools is corporate ethics," Dale Horowitz told one such group. "You are about to undergo a grueling and costly course of study, and there are many who would give anything to be in your place. You can expect us to be loyal to you, but we would like to think that you will return that loyalty. Sad to say, some of you will leave after a year or so and never look back." Gutfreund said the same thing in a more oblique fashion: "My senior associates and I have a very difficult task here in trying to manage the very talented young members of the firm whose intellects are developing rapidly."[18] This concern on his part was one of the main motivations for action taken after he became the CEO.

Defections of younger members were not the only problem. The unsettling of the partnership started in 1978, when Jay Perry went to Dean Witter Reynolds after being on the losing end of a brief power struggle at headquarters.

In 1979, Edgar Aronson switched to Dillon, Read to head the international department. In 1980, Vincent Murphy took a position at Merrill Lynch in the real estate and mortgage areas. Others followed, and the spring of 1981 saw an intensification of the talent drain.[19]

On May 11, 1981, Jim Wolfensohn announced he would resign as of the first of October. Wolfensohn's reputation had grown greatly as a result of his effective work at Salomon Brothers, so much so that he was being talked about as a possible successor to Robert McNamara as president of the World Bank. However, Wolfensohn had devoted much of his time to one single project, the Chrysler rescue, and his attention to corporate finance consequently suffered. This caused grumbling among those partners who were anxious for the entire range of activities in that field to expand. Moreover, it was bandied about that several of Wolfensohn's friends wanted to back him in an independent venture. In addition, he was deeply involved with the Carnegie Hall Corporation, of which he was chairman.[20]

Wolfensohn had hired Harold Tanner as his assistant at Salomon Brothers. Previously Tanner had been in corporate finance at Blyth Eastman Dillon, and more and more of Wolfensohn's managerial responsibilities in this area were being delegated to him. Therefore, the news of Wolfensohn's departure did not come as a great surprise, except that it sparked talk about a change at Salomon Brothers not unrelated to that October 1 date. In fact, Gutfreund was considering a major move to help stanch the outflow of talent.

This time a Wall Street rumor proved to be correct. In the summer of 1981, Salomon Brothers entered into merger discussions with an interested partner, Phibro Corp. Listed on the NYSE, Phibro was an international house trading more than 160 different commodities in 45 countries on all continents. The merger was officially announced on August 3, 1981, to take effect October 1.

With revenues of $23.6 billion, Phibro was a huge, energetic company. Formerly known as Philipp Brothers, the firm's greatest period of growth began in the 1950s, when the combination of expanding world trade and the executive direction of Ludwig Jesselson enabled the firm to emerge as one of the world's major trading operations. Jesselson's finest coup was to place Philipp Brothers into petroleum trading in the early 1970s, shortly before the 1973 OPEC oil embargo. By 1981, petroleum provided the firm with more than half its revenues — reminiscent of Salomon Brothers' good timing in its move into mortgage-backed securities.

In 1960, Philipp Brothers was throwing off large profits, more than required for its operations, and it needed a place to invest some of its funds. That year it merged with Minerals & Chemicals Corp. of America (M&C), a publicly owned entity that mined a variety of nonmetallic minerals. Another motive was that the partners' funds had been tied up in the then privately owned Philipp Brothers, and with the merger they now had M&C shares that could be sold. By doing this, Jesselson and the other partners could convert their equity into cash before the next economic downturn.

In 1967 the firm merged with Engelhard Industries, a fabricator of and dealer in precious metals, to form Engelhard Minerals & Chemicals. Once again there was talk of the marvels of synergy. The idea was for Philipp Brothers to market the raw materials turned out by Engelhard along with those of M&C, but the merger worked out badly. Milton Rosenthal of M&C later observed that his firm and Engelhard were constantly making long term decisions and commitments, while Philipp Brothers was concerned with trading, which involved a shorter time frame.

Engelhard was led by the mysterious Charles Engelhard (who was the model for Ian Fleming's James Bond archvillain, Auric Goldfinger), a high-living devotee of the good life and a fixture in the international horse breeding and racing set. The Philipp traders were a rough-and-ready lot, independent souls who were further distressed when Engelhard sold a 30 percent interest in the firm to the South African Harry Oppenheimer's Mineral & Resources (Minorco), a worldwide investment firm. This was a prelude to a split in the company, which came in early 1981, when Phibro (as Philipp Brothers then became named) became an entity separate from Engelhard. Each was pleased, but especially the Phibro group, since at the time they were a robust, expanding operation, accounting for around 90 percent of the Englehard profits.[21]

In 1981, Phibro was headed by David Tendler, a City College of New York graduate who had joined the firm some twenty years earlier. He started in the mail room, rose to trader and then moved on up the slippery pole to become Jesselson's heir apparent. "You're talking about a guy who is a first-generation survival type from the streets," said one of Tendler's associates. "He'll listen if you're in a real jam. But if you try to chisel him, you're dead. *Dead.*" As for the company itself, Phibro was composed of a group of sharp and successful traders known for their commitment to obtaining and retaining business. "They may not play dirty tricks," said a former trader there, "but they'll throw a lot of curves and spitballs. They are always looking for weaknesses in your position. They never take anything for granted. They may be very big, but they are still very hungry."[22]

Tendler and Gutfreund were familiar with each other's companies, but Gutfreund probably had the edge in this, since Salomon Brothers had functioned as one of Phibro's investment bankers. Indeed, Gutfreund recalled selling Philipp tax-exempts when he was a trader back in the 1950s. Salomon Brothers had served as Philipp Brothers' advisor during the split with Engelhard, and in 1981 was an important marketer of Phibro's commercial paper.

Tendler broached the subject to Gutfreund in a breakfast meeting in January 1981. Each firm manifestly had a great deal to offer the other. Tendler appeared to be transforming Phibro from a commodities firm into a merchant bank. He had already begun by establishing a Swiss bank, and the merger with Salomon Brothers was a logical next step in this direction.

Phibro was financing mining ventures in return for the right to market their output, and this was very close to investment banking. It was an idea that was being much discussed in the district. Other commodities and financial houses soon entered similar discussions. The results included the takeover by Goldman, Sachs of J. Aron, and Donaldson, Lufkin & Jenrette's acquisition of ACLI International.

These moves made sense to the commodities people, who felt that money was just another vehicle to trade. But Tendler was thinking ahead to commodity-backed bonds issued by governments with shaky finances and to other ventures. The union with Salomon, he said, "gives us the ultimate, limitless world to trade — money — while we are in the finite world of commodities, where the supply is limited."

What might Salomon Brothers gain from such a merger? An injection of capital from Phibro could provide Salomon with the kinds of funds needed to make even stronger bids in growing areas of opportunity such as domestic and foreign investment banking and mortgage-backed securities. As one observer noted later on, it was a marriage of "Salomon's ingenuity with Phibro's cash."[23]

"The main consideration was the capital base," commented William Vouté, a managing director and recently selected member of the Salomon Brothers' Executive Committee. "We saw the size of the market expanding and the U.S. Treasury needs expanding. We had only in the neighborhood of $300 million in capital, and it was felt that this wasn't enough to bring us into the next century."[24]

Gutfreund thought commodities would experience faster growth in the 1980s than securities would, and this view was supported by Henry Kaufman, whose role in management was growing. While Salomon Brothers' partners had scanty knowledge of commodities, they shared Phibro's attitude of the similarities in trading techniques and objectives. "What we've done is leapfrog 20 years ahead," Gutfreund remarked when the negotiations were completed. "It explodes the size of our universe."

In addition, Phibro's unparalleled international experience could serve Salomon Brothers well. "We both have an international outlook," said Gutfreund. "Money and commodities are interchangeable in many respects and are interrelated in the cash and futures markets." Or at least, so it appeared at the time.[25]

The merger, fashioned by Salomon Brothers' Richard Rosenthal and Ira Harris with Tendler and Phibro's president Hal Beretz, accomplished for Salomon Brothers what the union with Minerals & Chemicals had for Phibro a generation earlier.

It enabled Gutfreund and the other partners to take their money out of the firm at a time when the entire industry was churning and turning. As a former employee would remark, "Playing the game with somebody else's money has a way of making life more relaxed."[26]

There was one additional aspect to the merger that may have eluded some financial journalists and other observers. One of the basic rules of investment is that rewards can come in two forms, dividends and interest as well as capital gains. The former are paid out by the company, the latter are produced by the market. As a partnership Salomon Brothers could only reward its personnel with bonuses and interest, but as a publicly owned entity the firm could tie remuneration to the market price of its shares.

Richard G. Rosenthal   J. Ira Harris

Under a complex plan worked out by Ira Harris, Salomon Brothers created a "phantom pool" of 1.2 million shares of Phibro common stock at an established price of $30 per share. These shares were awarded to key personnel and some of the more junior partners. The arrangement was to last for five years, and in 1986 the holders would receive in cash the number of units times the highest price the shares reached during that period. Assume, for example, that at the end of five years the stock was selling for 10, but at one point it had reached 50. The owner of 10,000 units would then receive a cash payment of $500,000. "I think that's a pretty good piece of glue," reflected Gutfreund. "One of the things we'll have to continue to think about and work on is that we maintain our competitive compensation situation. Not just for one year, but continually."[27]

By merging with Phibro, Salomon Brothers not only enlarged its capital and horizons, but hoped to resolve the problem of retaining valued professionals.

The price paid by Phibro for Salomon Brothers was set at $550 million in cash and securities. Salomon Brothers' partners would withdraw their capital, which came to $300 million, to be replaced by Phibro. In addition, the general partners would receive $250 million in 9 percent notes convertible into common stock at $27.78.

The holding company of Phibro-Salomon was to be created under the new arrangement, with Tendler and Gutfreund as its co-chairmen. Gutfreund, Horowitz, Kaufman, Schmeelk, Harris and Rosenthal joined the board of the newly established Phibro-Salomon.

There were several important signs that Tendler and Phibro were to lead the combine. Phibro's Hal Beretz became president and chief operating officer. Tendler took a seat on the Salomon Brothers Executive Committee, and there was no Salomon Brothers representative on the Philipp Brothers board. Of Phibro-Salomon's thirteen vice presidents only five came from Salomon. The primacy extended to symbols as well. In the first Annual Report, Tendler and Gutfreund were listed as co-chairmen, but not in alphabetical order as was customary; Tendler's name came first.

Despite the talk of cooperation it was soon evident that there would be less of it than originally expected. Both co-chairmen were aggressive and ambitious, each was proud of his company and certain it was the better of the two in the marriage. Observers in both industries agreed that there would be friction. Asked his opinion of Phibro, Henry Jarecki of Mocatta Metals replied, "They will chew you up and spit you out." Another observer said, "When Tendler and Gutfreund eat together, they ought to bring along two food tasters. I think it's already time to start placing bets." But since the stakes were high, self-interest dictated cooperation.

An unnamed investment banker involved in the transaction observed: "Phibro's business is changing radically from just buying and selling commodities to one in which they must be there from day one on mine projects and the like in order to lock in an assured supply." With Salomon Brothers, he thought, "they are [now] better able to do this than anyone else in the world."[28]

The bets were already in place that autumn, and most were on Tendler, who was younger, brasher, and seemed hungrier than Gutfreund. Tendler continued to talk expansively of the future, while Gutfreund was becoming more reflective and, if anything, demonstrated candor regarding his view of himself in the new arrangement. To a reporter's observation that he didn't appear to be too comfortable in management, Gutfreund replied, "Frankly, I would rather write a ticket in the trading room than manage. Of course, I don't write tickets anymore, and there are very few areas where I would be competent to do so." And he sounded like an elder statesman when adding, "While I do enjoy the management role, it's because I feel a challenge, not because I think it's the most gratifying job in the world. The world of finance can, on occasion, involve us in the highest calling. From time to time we have had the opportunity to influence society in a favorable way."[29]

The merger became effective on October 1, 1981 — the date Jim Wolfensohn had set for his retirement five months earlier, prior to the announcement of the merger talks. The atmosphere was settled and calm at One New York Plaza, as it was at Phibro's headquarters at 1221 Avenue of the Americas. There were the usual pleasantries and congratulations, but also some suggestion of tension. "Did you ever go to a wedding where the bride's family decided it didn't like the groom's, and vice versa. Well, that was what it was like," said an unidentified Salomon Brothers managing director, who added, "And don't forget, this isn't the groom's first marriage."

Chapter X

The Promise of the Future 1980-1984

The reputation of Salomon Brothers as an imaginative, innovative, and expanding investment banker was recognized in the district and the entire financial world well before the 1980s. However, the most sanguine observer could not have predicted the veritable explosion of activity which occurred from 1982 to 1984. It was coincidental that the firm's immense growth came at the time of the merger with Phibro, and yet both parties were greatly affected by it in ways not clearly foreseen when they originally joined together.

What remained constant was the successful management system at Salomon Brothers. Led by John Gutfreund, the Executive Committee managed change in a highly successful way. It brought a stability that tempered the constant flow of ideas and proposals bubbling up through the ranks without stifling that valuable flow. Each member of the committee pursued responsibilities that were in line with his experience and expertise. Gutfreund drew particularly on the wisdom of Henry Kaufman. Dr. Kaufman had brought the firm renown for his expert knowledge of the financial markets, but he proved to be an able executive as well. This was demonstrated first in his development of the research group and later in quietly helping Gutfreund to deal with the various issues that have been central to the firm's success. He has been particularly helpful in such areas as overall management of risk taking, employment policies and practices, and — most vital of all — maintaining the ethos and integrity of the firm. The constancy provided by the Executive Committee, and the management concept it represents, are crucial elements in keeping Salomon Brothers on the path to investment banking leadership.

This leadership became increasingly evident during the years immediately preceding the 75th anniversary of Salomon Brothers. It was a fertile period in which the firm's expertise was applied in diverse ways to help corporate treasurers and government ministers to raise the funds they needed in a challenging marketplace where interest rates were both high and volatile. It also was a time when the mergers and acquisitions business came into full flower and when Salomon's experts were called on to play a crucial role in the biggest rescue operation in industrial history, the salvation of Chrysler. The mortgage market, patiently cultivated since 1978, finally became recognized as a major new province of the capital markets. And the marketplace itself was revolutionized by a new procedure, sanctioned by the SEC, that speeded the flow of securities from issuers to investors. It was a time of great ferment, and most of the change was in directions thoroughly compatible with capabilities Salomon Brothers had fashioned over the previous seven decades.

Increasing demands upon money markets in the early eighties led the firm to originate new securities and investment techniques to meet the ever more complex requirements of the era. For example, institutional investors shied away from certain types of debt and other types of investments when interest rates were uncertain, encouraging investment bankers to develop instruments that could be placed at lower rates. In 1980, Salomon created a novel bond for a sovereign nation which featured an attached warrant. This was the $200 million, 13.65 percent, five-year Kingdom of Sweden issue with warrants enabling the holder to purchase an additional note within six months under the same terms. It was marketed at a time when notes of a similar quality were fetching around 14.3 percent, and Sweden was saved about $6 million in interest costs.

The success of the Swedish issue prompted a flood of similar underwritings by other firms. Still, Salomon Brothers led in this innovative area of financing. In another case, the firm organized a syndicate offering $100 million in Municipal Assistance Corporation (MAC) bonds to mature in 2008, and having a detachable warrant which would save MAC approximately $17 million over the life of the bonds.

Salomon Brothers further pioneered in the burgeoning area of Original Issue Discount (OID) bonds. These bonds sold below par, provided the holder with call protection and tax benefits, and thus could be sold at lower rates. The first of these issues was a $150 million, 5⅞ percent convertible debenture for Dana Corporation that was floated in 1981. It had a 2006 maturity and was priced at 50 to yield 12.387 percent to maturity.

The success of this new form of instrument encouraged the creation of others. Salomon Brothers marketed the Money Market Multiplier zero coupon notes and the Certificates of Accrual on Treasury Securities (CATS®). The latter were created by stripping coupons from Treasury bonds and selling them as zero coupon bonds. While other investment banks dealt in similar securities, the Salomon Brothers version became the most popular of the group.

Certificates of Accrual on Treasury Securities (CATS®) were listed in 1982, combining the features of zero-coupon investments with the quality of U.S. Treasury issues.

In another venture, Salomon Brothers, working with corporate treasurers, devised a swap technique that provided its clients with an important measure of liquidity and helped strengthen their balance sheets. When the bond market reached an historic low in the late 1970s due to soaring interest rates, Salomon Brothers purchased deeply discounted bonds for a client. The firm then exchanged these bonds for newly issued common shares, a procedure which became commonly known as a "debt for equity swap."

In this swap, the client firm's interest charges declined, often by substantially more than the higher dividend requirements, so that earnings improved, and the entire operation was tax-free. Salomon Brothers acted as an intermediary at risk, because the price of the common stock it received in exchange for the bonds might decline prior to their sale. "We structured ourselves as a principal, and we were very much at risk in the marketplace," noted Salomon Brothers vice president Warren Foss, Jr. "We get paid in shares of stock, and whether or not we make or lose money is a function of how we distribute the stock."

For example, acting for Quaker Oats in August 1981, Salomon Brothers purchased $14 million par value of the firm's 7.7 percent debentures from institutional investors, and then two weeks later exchanged them for 288,000 shares of common stock. That same day Salomon Brothers resold the shares at a 4 percent premium. As a result, Quaker Oats' debt was reduced by $14 million, and the company had a $4.9 million tax-free extraordinary gain. "We do two things for a corporation," Foss observed. "First, we help them extinguish debt in a tax-free method, and second, we help them get around the difficult problems of an equity base that has not kept pace with growing debt."[1]

The success of this offering led to additional swaps; in fact, a total of 19 in the next four months alone, including deals for Duke Power, Crown Zellerbach, Western Union, and Procter and Gamble. "There is a very active level of interest," said Salomon vice president Thomas McCaughey. "In defeasance we don't have to negotiate with individual bondholders, so the company can retire the entire issue."[2]

In 1982, the Financial Accounting Standards Board attempted to prohibit firms from avoiding or deferring taxes, which led to a reduction in the popularity of defeasance, and this resulted in a temporary decline in activity. But Salomon Brothers and others developed variations which muted some criticisms, and swaps continued. In all, these innovative techniques provided corporate treasurers with much desired flexibility in a difficult financial environment.[3]

One of the more common buzzwords of the early 1980s was "leveraged" buyouts, in which the purchaser uses the assets of the firm he is acquiring in order to pay for part of its cost. Salomon Brothers engaged in its share of these, but at the same time developed novel variations. One of these was for Esmark, which asked Salomon Brothers to come up with a plan for its employees to purchase its fresh meat operations. Drawing upon the combined talents of the Mergers and Acquisitions Group of its Corporate Finance, Equity Sales, and Syndicate Departments, Salomon created Swift Independent Corporation (SIPCO) and made a public offering of the new entity's stock. The syndicate offered 2.75 million shares at $15, raising some $41 million, and these funds made SIPCO's creation possible.

The mortgage area continued to be fertile, and by 1984 mortgage-backed securities were acknowledged to be one of the most lucrative investment instruments created in a generation. Gutfreund noted that there were $1.3 trillion in residential mortgages, of which only $250 billion had been securitized, but that the amount was growing. A decade earlier thrifts held mortgages as investments; in more recent times they have sold off their mortgages and purchased highly liquid mortgage-based securities for their portfolios. Approximately 40 percent of all home mortgages issued during 1983 were securitized, and Salomon Brothers was trading them at the rate of $15 billion a month.[4]

By then Robert Dall had stepped down for reasons of health, and Gutfreund selected Lewis Ranieri to succeed him as head of the mortgage securities and real estate activities. Under Ranieri's guidance Salomon Brothers led in the creation of mortgage innovations, including the collateralized mortgage obligation (CMO), an instrument which enabled investors to select securities representing early, middle, or late maturities from a single pool. This came in response to the most often heard criticism of mortgage securities, namely, that their uncertain lifespan made them less desirable than bonds. In its first year, Freddie Mac sold approximately $10 billion worth of CMOs, and Salomon Brothers accounted for close to 65 percent of the total.

The mortgage-backed securities market grew very rapidly, to the extent that in 1983 investors purchased $89 billion of them, an increase from the previous year's sales of $54 billion. The firm continued to increase the variety of instruments, including the creation of securities backed by commercial mortgages. By 1984, Ranieri and his group were trading and selling 27 different kinds of products, most of which had been devised by Salomon Brothers. Ranieri was appointed to the Executive Committee at the beginning of that year, a logical promotion in view of the fact that mortgage securities reputedly accounted for a significant portion of the firm's profits for the previous year.[5]

Meanwhile, there had been a landmark development in the way the capital markets work, and it seemed tailored to the firm's special qualities. The Securities and Exchange Commission was considering changes in the methods by which securities were registered prior to offering. Until then, the registration process had been extremely lengthy. A firm would commission an underwriter directly. Then, decisions about the nature and size of the offering would be made by the client and its investment bank. Next, a prospectus would be drawn up and pricing arrangements selected. This process often took several months to complete, and during that time the company and its bank would have to be in constant touch.

In 1982, the SEC was pondering a revised system making it possible for a corporation to register in advance all the securities it intended to issue over the next two-year span. Then the corporation could offer any of them in literally a matter of hours. A company might have in readiness an issue of, say, $100 million in 20-year debentures, and bring it to market at a time when rates and acceptance seemed best. Moreover, it could do so through an underwriter or institution selected at the last minute (which would subject the industry to even more intense competition), or it could sell directly to an investment institution.

The investment banking community was quick to grasp the implications of such a change. Under such a rule, a corporation might solicit interest from several underwriters, list all or none of them on the prospectus, and make them compete against one another. Under this system, underwriters who were not alert could lose clients to hungrier and more aggressive houses. The big firms were rather displeased with the idea, and even some of the smaller ones were dubious. The real winners, of course, would be the corporations whose securities were being offered. Whether it was in the public interest was certainly debatable. To cite the most obvious problem, such offerings would hardly allow sufficient time for the public to evaluate disclosure with sufficient care and analysis.

Nevertheless, the concept, soon to be known as "Shelf Registration" (since the firm was taking its issue off the shelf when sold) under the SEC's Rule 415, was enacted in early 1982 on a trial basis. An uproar was set off on the Street. "We're moving from the traditional concept of marriage to one-night stands," mused Frederick Friswold of Dain Bosworth. John Whitehead of Goldman, Sachs was livid, warning that Rule 415 "threatens to sweep away 50 years of investor protection and return the new-issues market to the jungle environment of the 1920s."[6]

John Gutfreund testified before the SEC on the matter in June, 1982. The new competition unleashed by Rule 415 didn't bother him as much as other aspects of the change. "I don't want to depend on a self-interested party, namely, the corporate issuers of America, for the best possible disclosure to investors. I think their objective, which is to raise capital at the cheapest possible price, may not be in the interest of the public investor." In Gutfreund's view, the rapidity of the offerings might not give investors time to ponder decisions. "The so-called need for instant access to the market, what I call the window philosophy, is a confusion of priorities. The question is not whether an issuer pays a little more or less for his capital. The concern is whether he has a sound business venture."[7]

Activity at the syndicate desk was hectic as Salomon Brothers became the worldwide leader in underwriting securities.

Despite such misgivings, Salomon Brothers prospered in the increasingly deregulated environment that was then developing. In order to succeed under Rule 415, underwriters had to hone their sensitivity to the market and be prepared often to commit large sums on very short notice. This had traditionally been one of the firm's fortes, and Salomon Brothers skillfully enlarged its share of underwritings.

In 1983, the first full year for the new system, shelf registrations accounted for 38 percent of all underwriting volume, and Salomon Brothers was the industry's leader, participating in 170 issues which raised $16.5 billion. Contrary to expectations, the market share of the top half dozen firms actually increased, rising to 43 percent from 26 percent in debt and to 32 percent from 16 percent in equities.

Salomon Brothers' position in other areas of corporate finance was expanding as well. The firm was retained as advisor by American Telephone & Telegraph in what was to be the largest and most important corporate breakup in American history, involving the divestiture of assets of over $100 billion and the emergence of a new AT&T. Among the larger merger and acquisition deals, the firm advised Xerox on its acquisition of Crum & Foster, Santa Fe Industries on its merger with the Southern Pacific Company, Gulf Oil on its combination with Standard Oil of California (Chevron), and the J. Paul Getty Trust when Getty Oil was acquired by Texaco.[8] In 1984 alone, Salomon Brothers was involved in mergers at a rate of better than one per week. The firm also continued to offer financial counsel and support to distressed companies, including AM International, International Harvester, Parsons & Whittemore, and the Lionel Corporation.

The most dramatic and important advice and assistance given by the firm was in the Chrysler Corporation rescue, though, of course, Salomon Brothers operated as part of a team in this instance. The U.S. and Canadian governments, the United Auto Workers, hundreds of suppliers, and a large number of banks were all directly involved. However, at the crucial moment Salomon Brothers provided Chrysler with vitally important financial credibility, and in the process put itself at considerable risk.

Salomon Brothers' involvement with Chrysler came about in an indirect fashion. In July 1978, Lee Iacocca was fired as president of Ford Motors and was looking for other employment opportunities. For a while he considered organizing an international firm, comprised of several existing operations, such as Chrysler, American Motors, Volkswagen, and perhaps Fiat or Renault. The result would be what Iacocca called "Global Motors," an entity capable of competing with the major Japanese firms, General Motors and Ford.

Iacocca approached John Gutfreund with the idea, asking him to conduct a feasibility study, which was initiated in the autumn of 1978. Not aware of Iacocca's activities after his dismissal, Chrysler contacted him in October to explore whether he would be interested in joining that firm. The hope was that Iacocca, who was considered one of the industry's ablest executives, could duplicate at Chrysler some of the success he had achieved at Ford. Chrysler chairman John Riccardo and president Eugene Cafiero were surprised at the breadth and depth of his knowledge of the company in their discussions with him. Then they learned of the Salomon input.

"He knows more about us than we do," Riccardo told one of his executives afterwards. "He's had Salomon Brothers do some work on us."[9] Iacocca agreed to come to Chrysler, ultimately as chairman and chief executive officer. He naturally turned to the services of Salomon Brothers in his new job.

Chrysler was falling ever deeper into trouble in 1979, a time when most American firms were suffering from the triple blows of the second oil shock, a recession, and competition from Japanese automobile manufacturers. Under Iacocca the firm was attempting to remain afloat while preparing new, and hopefully popular, entries for the coming model year. But the Chrysler deficit in 1979 came to more than $1 billion, and it was evident that matters would worsen in the immediate future. The corporation clearly was not going to be able to survive without a good deal of financial assistance.

A Salomon Brothers team, working in conjunction with consultants from Booz, Allen & Hamilton, prepared a detailed report, predicting the 1979 loss almost to the dollar. The report went on to say that there might be a loss of as much as $482 million in 1980, but that Chrysler could return to profitability in 1981.

The Salomon Brothers people involved with Chrysler also assisted in preparing the case for presentation to congressmen who might approve a proposed federal rescue mission in mid-December. While debates were raging in the House of Representatives, Salomon Brothers observed that the corporation might run out of money as early as January 15, 1980, and that immediate action was imperative if it were to be successful. The rescue plan was approved. There would be federal loan guarantees of $1.5 billion, and the government would receive warrants to purchase 14.4 million shares of Chrysler common stock. The United Auto Workers granted concessions which amounted to $5,000 per worker, which enabled Chrysler to have the lowest labor costs at that time of any North American auto manufacturer.

Other cuts followed, and the Canadian government, 150-odd banks and Chrysler's suppliers all granted concessions. Private lenders agreed to accept preferred stock as payment for $1.1 billion in outstanding debt, to be turned in for cash a year after Chrysler repaid its government-guaranteed loans. Never before had any American corporation received so massive an infusion of funds and credit.

Even so, it did not seem that it would be sufficient. The auto market proved weaker than Salomon Brothers had anticipated, and Chrysler's losses for 1980 came to $1.7 billion. Indeed, every American auto maker was in the red that year — there was some question not only of Chrysler's survival, but also that of American Motors and even Ford.

This situation called for a bold approach, and Iacocca and Salomon Brothers' James Wolfensohn came up with one. They considered a merger between Ford and Chrysler to form a firm capable of giving strong competition to General Motors and the Japanese. Wolfensohn approached Ford through its investment banker, Goldman, Sachs, which in turn brought the idea to Ford's management. There the suggestion was dismissed out of hand. The idea was dropped, for as Iacocca remarked, "We don't go to parties we're not invited to."[10]

By 1982, it had become obvious that Chrysler was recovering, but financial problems remained, one being the preferred stock that had been issued to the lenders. "We had to get rid of that preferred stock," recalled Chrysler's executive vice president for finance Robert S. Miller. "It was a disincentive for our ever repaying the government." Unless the government loans were eliminated, Chrysler would evolve into a federally dependent operation, and that would have important and dangerous implications for the very future of capitalism in America.[11]

Miller and David Schulte, a Salomon Brothers vice president working out of the Chicago office, developed an intriguing plan. They would attempt to convince the owners of the preferred shares to exchange them for common shares, with the understanding that Salomon Brothers would make this arrangement more attractive by undertaking a forward underwriting to pre-sell some of the common to other investors.

Negotiations began in late 1982, with First Boston representing the creditors and Salomon Brothers the corporation. In January 1983, Miller and Schulte suggested reclassifying the $1.1 billion in preferred into 29.15 million shares of common. This would be conditional on the willingness of financial institutions that owned warrants to tender 80 percent of them at the rate of one share of common for 1.7 warrants. The offer was accepted, and all depended upon Salomon Brothers being able to place the shares successfully.

At the time, a Chrysler common share was selling at around 18, having risen on good corporate news from its bottom of 3½ a year earlier. Thus, there was bound to be interest in the secondary issue, though taking so many shares to market at once could depress the price of the stock unless handled carefully. Originally Salomon Brothers had intended to offer 10 million shares, but investor interest and the by-now legendary placement power of the firm enabled it to increase the underwriting to 26 million shares. Amazingly, the issue was sold out in two hours, and $432 million was raised for the corporation.

Still later in 1983, Salomon Brothers represented Chrysler in talks with the federal government regarding the options it held. The firm advised Iacocca to purchase the options at the scheduled auction, and helped structure the bid. Chrysler was consequently able to retire the warrants, and in such a way that dilution of its equity was avoided, and the government loan guarantee was rewarded.[12]

While Salomon Brothers was performing impressive feats for clients, it had become apparent by 1984 that the firm's most far-reaching transaction — its merger with Phibro — was not turning out as well as the Executive Committee had anticipated. Part of the reason was the recession, which impacted severely upon the commodities markets in which Phibro was the leader. Stated simply, many of the markets fell apart. "You know how long I've been at Phibro?" asked Ludwig Jesselson in early 1983. "Forty-five years. And I have *never* experienced as disastrous a situation in our commodities as I've experienced during the last two years." To which a sympathetic John Gutfreund commented that the results of the first year of the merger were "disappointing.... It's been a very, very difficult year for Philipp Brothers.... I think you have to give them some time.... I don't want to make a quick judgment."[13]

Salomon Brothers reported pre-tax earnings of $350 million in 1982, while Phibro's came to $173 million, leading a large number of analysts to second-guess Gutfreund on the terms of the deal. Salomon Brothers' earnings soared in 1983 to a record $415 million, while Phibro's came in at $260 million. Once again the Salomon people were criticized for accepting so low a price back in the Fall of 1981, but this time critics failed to realize that a change had taken place in the relationship between the two parts of the firm.

In 1983, Ben Bollag, a Phibro executive who recently had left the firm, told a reporter that the marriage was bound to be stormy, but that in his view Salomon would become the dominant force, and not because of the power of its markets relative to those of Philipp. "My prediction is that it's a matter of time before the Salomon team is going to be running Phibro." The reason, he said, was "Salomon's professional management," which Bollag thought superior to that of Phibro.[14]

Whether or not this was so is moot, but as so often is the case in finance, power followed earnings. The leadership of Gutfreund and the Executive Committee, the enhanced capital base and the firm's skills in a rapidly changing marketplace all combined to produce outstanding results. Salomon Brothers proved to be the superior money maker during the first two years of the merger, and the performance of the firm placed it on the ascendancy in its relations with Phibro.

That this was so became indisputably evident in the spring of 1984, when rumors regarding readjustments at the firm were heard. The news broke on May 22, when Phibro-Salomon confirmed that it was "studying the possibility" of selling all of the Philipp Brothers' commodities business, minus its oil operations, to David Tendler and a group of executives at Phibro. While the news gave the market and Phibro-Salomon stock a jolt, it was not, as indicated, a complete surprise. "Maybe the idea of commodity trading and banking looked good at the time," remarked one industry observer, "but the meshing didn't take place. By its nature, maybe, commodity trading would be better as a private business than a public one."[15]

The following day, Donaldson, Lufkin & Jenrette announced a plan to sell its commodities operation, ACLI

International, showing that the disappointment with that business hardly was unique to Phibro-Salomon. But in the uncertainty that followed, the price of the Phibro-Salomon stock fell sharply, only to rise a week later when the company announced the plan was being abandoned. The speculation was that Tendler was unable to raise sufficient funds, estimated at between $1.25 billion and $2.5 billion. In addition, the Phibro group would have had to develop a $3 billion line of credit in order to maintain operations, and this too was not forthcoming.

The buyout attempt had its ironic side. Two and a half years earlier Salomon had been private and Phibro public; had the buyout worked as planned, the roles would have been reversed. As it was, the collapse of the buyout plan enhanced Gutfreund's stature and influence. Given a continued world economic recovery, some argued, Philipp Brothers would show excellent earnings, in which case it could become dominant once again; but whether or not this would transpire had to be judged against the excellent prospects of Salomon in the same period. An unnamed executive at a competing firm was quoted in *The Wall Street Journal* as saying, "You can't put Humpty-Dumpty together again. Sooner or later the companies will split up."[16]

On August 6, 1984, the firm announced that while Gutfreund and Tendler would remain co-chairmen of Phibro-Salomon, in the future Gutfreund would be the sole chief executive officer, with Hal Beretz of Phibro serving as president and chief operating officer. Gutfreund tried to downplay the significance of the change. "This is an evolutionary move. In no way should this be read as reducing the emphasis on our historical businesses." But rumors persisted that a divorce was in the works. On October 5, *The Wall Street Journal* reported that the firm had announced the layoff of 65 Philipp Brothers employees in the New York office and another 50 worldwide due to the decline in business. That same day Tendler and Beretz announced their resignations, and the firm elevated Alan Flacks of Phibro to fill their places. Gutfreund told the press, "I understand and respect their decisions to resign. We are grateful for all of their efforts in the years past and wish them every success." Tendler talked of Phibro-Salomon's "exciting future," and indicated Flacks' appointment "augurs well for everyone in our company."[17]

After a quick but thorough study of their operations, Gutfreund began reorganizing the management structures of Philipp Brothers and Phibro Energy along the lines tested and proven through decades of experience at Salomon Brothers.

Phibro Corporation
has changed its name to

PHIBRO-SALOMON INC

New ticker symbol:
PSB (NYSE)

Philipp Brothers, Inc.
Worldwide marketing
of raw materials.

Salomon Brothers Inc
International investment banking
and securities trading.

In 1981 Salomon Brothers combined with Phibro to form Phibro-Salomon Inc, bringing an infusion of capital into Salomon Brothers that allowed for even further expansion in such areas as domestic and foreign investment banking and mortgage-backed securities.

Having perceived earlier the similarities in the Phibro and Salomon businesses, he now saw how similar management concepts could be applied successfully.

Whatever transpires next in this tempestuous marriage, Salomon Brothers' power and prestige on the Street and in its field remain unquestioned. In 1984, the firm was worldwide leader in underwriting securities, raising over $150 billion. Trading and sales reached $2.4 trillion, and total capital of the Salomon Brothers group was $1.7 billion at the end of the year. Three-quarters of a century from the time that three brothers and their clerk decided to set out on their own in a small corner of the financial marketplace, Salomon Brothers was the leading investment banker in many areas of its operations and among the top firms in virtually all of them. In this situation, John Gutfreund's responsibilities as CEO were enormously expanded and placed him in a pivotal position in the world of international finance.

Chapter XI

The Salomon Ethos

What ingredients have been gathered to result in Salomon Brothers' dynamic leadership within the financial area? Many different elements have been involved. First, the building of capital obviously has been vital. In addition, research, under Henry Kaufman, has had an increasingly important role, as have the firm's marketing sensitivities which were developed over many years of experience in sales and trading. Most important, however, have been the people. The cumulative experience and principles of people who have worked or now work at Salomon Brothers have created an ethos that guides the firm, explains its success and charts its future course.

The self-perpetuating Salomon style, or ethos, is worth examining, both for what it explains about the past and present and for what it promises in the future. John Gutfreund has made evident in striking fashion his concept of just what that is, both through his actions in restructuring the firm and by sharpening and articulating its focus.

As has been noted, one of Gutfreund's most important priorities when he assumed leadership of Salomon Brothers in 1978 was to devise new strategies for the firm in a changing financial and social world, then to create a new type of structure to carry them forward. The merger with Phibro took the company public and increased its capital substantially, and this has proved to be a major strategic move. "The impact of what we did was far greater than anything I ever expected," Gutfreund remarked in 1985. "At the time, we did not fully anticipate the enormous impact that would be felt when we multiplied our capital by five or six times — what that would do with the business. That's why I say the past is rather important to judge the future."[1]

Insofar as structure is concerned, Gutfreund notes that further integration of operating units can be expected and that expansion into new activities will continue, as

Salomon Brothers stands prepared to react to the rapidly evolving marketplace and serve its clients. "But we aren't going to move people in a hurry. We think that when the individuals — who in every way are the keys to this business — respect each other and understand the disciplines, they will do very well supporting each other." Central organization will be strengthened, to deal with so complex a structure, but it will not be done at the expense of stifling initiative and individuality.

"If things work here, it's not because I dictate them," Gutfreund adds. "Things work because the people in trading and sales come up with ideas they think make sense, and want to carry them out. We get the right person for the job. Rarely does anything happen because management decides something ought to be done."

At the same time Gutfreund exerts a forceful yet flexible direction to keep all the components of the firm working together effectively and harmoniously. He sincerely feels that teamwork among independent individuals is the key to Salomon's successes. "I firmly believe that if I were to take an extended holiday of 10 days and something horrible were to happen, I'd have absolutely no doubt that the Executive Committee would meet on the matter and the appropriate senior person would make the final decision. Things happen all the time where members of the committee make decisions without me. I view the job structurally, as a matter of finding a harmony — as a conductor. I am not in a position of saying I am trying to run horse races. I hate to play that game, and I won't do it — pitting Mr. A. against Mr. B against Ms. C. That's nonsense."

Henry Kaufman agrees with this diagnosis, and is equally trenchant in analyzing the firm he entered almost a quarter of a century ago. Kaufman has isolated several prime characteristics that he feels make it unique, and he's created a statement of belief that helps guide Salomon Brothers as it positions itself for the future.

> Salomon Brothers, first of all, is a substantial market maker under all conditions. Whether prices are going up or prices are going sharply

lower, we are there to make the market. And we will put enormous amounts of capital at risk. That is one very important difference. We put substantial amounts of capital at risk in order to underwrite as well as to provide liquidity. I believe we do that more than anyone in the industry.

I also think that despite our growth we are an organization that has all of the various departments interlocked. We don't view ourselves as being in government securities and in corporate finance. We are part of an entity called Salomon Brothers. So there is an extraordinarily high degree of cooperation and coordination that takes place all the time, not on an intramarket basis, but intermarket, which I sense is far beyond anything else in the industry.

I also believe we continue to be a firm that is highly innovative in research. We constantly create new products, conduct fixed income investigation, and pioneer new trading techniques. Hopefully, we can continue to do this.

We have also been a leader in letting young people have the opportunity to really push ahead. This has been a recent trend in the Street, but we were there quite a long time ago. We put Lew Ranieri, a young fellow, into a very important position. And we were one of the few organizations in Wall Street that moved people along on the strength of their talent, not on their heritage.

Typically, Henry Kaufman's analysis ends with thoughts about people and their talents. His role in the growth of the firm has been important for several reasons and has made him a legendary figure in the district. He has often acted as spokesman for Salomon Brothers when the state of the market and the financial outlook for the country are being considered. His observations on investment trends and interest rates are heard around the world. At the same time he has been an active participant in the management of the firm, and his opinions are highly influential in the decision-making process of the Executive Committee.

Yet Salomon Brothers is not alone in having people of great talent. There are many elsewhere on Wall Street, and there is a great deal of mobility among firms. It is true, however, that veterans of the financial district recognize cultural differences among Salomon Brothers, First Boston, Morgan Stanley, Lazard Frères, Goldman, Sachs and Merrill Lynch, just to mention some major firms. These distinctions have existed in the past, and will surely continue into the future.

Much has been said about the contrasts between the old and the new establishments. Time has mitigated them to a large extent, and greater similarities appear among the third and fourth generations of Americans today than ever existed among their grandparents at the turn of the century. For example, someone who was applying for a job at Morgan Stanley in 1950 would probably not have considered seeking a position at Salomon Brothers. The two firms were worlds apart in social background, traditions and attitude. This no longer is true.

However, Salomon Brothers operates under several principles that help define the character and quality of the firm. One observes them in today's traders, salesmen and executives, and by analyzing them much can be understood about the Salomon ethos. They probably are expressed best by those who have come to understand them through their own experiences.

The first and foremost principle that new employees soon learn is that dedication to the client is all-important. Arthur Salomon said as much in 1910, and it remains true to this day. At Salomon Brothers the customer comes first, the firm second, and in time newcomers realize this is axiomatic. And the same phrase recurs: "We always try to make the customer whole."

Next, while ambition is respected and encouraged at Salomon Brothers, individuals are expected to function as members of a team. This includes not only everyone working at the home or domestic branch offices, but all those overseas as well. Teamwork is due, to a significant degree, to the firm's refusal to pay individual commissions, a concept of Arthur Salomon's which continues to this day and is almost unique in the district.

Executive Committee in 1984, responsible for the management of Salomon Brothers Inc, included (seated, from left) Gedale B. Horowitz, Richard J. Schmeelk, John H. Gutfreund, Henry Kaufman, and (standing, from left) Allan H. Fine, William J. Vouté, Lewis S. Ranieri, Thomas W. Strauss and James L. Massey.

A third operational principle is a strong belief in the virtues of meritocracy, as Kaufman has stressed. More than most firms in the district, Salomon prides itself on rewarding performance, not background. It is not at all unusual for individuals to become important traders and salesmen after starting out as clerks or trainees. Executive Committee members Gutfreund, Horowitz, Massey, Ranieri, Schmeelk, Strauss and Vouté are the most dramatic examples, but there are many more.

The fourth principle is that Salomon Brothers attracts, and is attracted by, individuals who have a hard-and-fast belief in the work ethic. New employees soon learn that Salomon expects total devotion. The people at Salomon work long hours, and often weekends as well. Gutfreund's 7:30 A.M. breakfast meetings are legendary in the district. Nevertheless, there are limits; the firm insists that vacations be taken, and not interrupted for business reasons. And when Henry Kaufman was asked in a televised interview what was paramount in his life, he answered without hesitation: "My family."

Teaching by example may be considered a fifth principle. It is combined with a mentor arrangement that has existed for years, and is a well-known hallmark of Salomon Brothers. Jonas Ottens, who had been with the firm from its earliest times, was famous for taking newcomers under his wing and instructing them in trading and sales techniques. This dedication of mentor to new employee amounts to almost a *mystique*. Virtually all the managers address the matter in one way or another. Gutfreund, who was guided by Ottens when he took over the syndication desk, recalled that Ottens "managed in a self-effacing, careful and thoughtful manner to teach me what I needed."

Sixth, and finally, the daily attitude around Salomon Brothers is present and future oriented. This is not surprising in an enterprise where, due to its rapid growth over the past decade, many managers are in their late twenties and early thirties, and where a person is regarded as a veteran if he or she has been on the job for more than five years. To them the distant future is next month, and the far past is the early

199

1980s, despite the fact that they are working with an ethos accumulated over 75 years.

Young people at Salomon Brothers are familiar with the generation which now directs the firm. In the nature of the fast-paced world in which they work, they are less aware of those who went before. They know rather little of the people who created the organization, led it through difficult periods, molded the foundation on which the present leaders built, and on which they will be expected to expand. Such an acquaintance with this heritage can only be beneficial, to them and to others with whom Salomon comes into contact.

"I came here in 1953," Dale Horowitz told a group of new employees, as he attempted to impress them with the changes which had transpired since then. "There were around 300 employees that year, and if we had five or six with postgraduate degrees, it was a lot. Most of the people who made this firm never even graduated from high school. Yet they had the instincts and intelligence to overcome some very tough situations. And this has left the firm with the most entrepreneurial spirit of any on Wall Street. I think that the present approaches come from the 300 who were here in the mid-1950s and, even more so, from the people who were here in the fifty years before that time. It has always been a firm where individual merit is crucial."

Horowitz paused for a question. One of his listeners, a trainee — this was in 1982 — wanted to know how this might change in the late 1980s, due to altered markets and the merger with Phibro. He clearly was interested more in where the firm was heading than how it had arrived where it was. Salomon Brothers was now his professional life, and he wanted to know what was in store for his future.

This present and future orientation is to be expected in an industry which is evolving so rapidly. Those who are committed so intensely to creating that future often have little time or interest in matters which do not bear directly on the challenges of the day. Yet, as Horowitz indicated, the history of this unique firm strongly influences not only its present but its future as well. If it is true that the past is prologue, in the case of Salomon Brothers it also is the continuing reality out of which success is generated.

This theme ran through John Gutfreund's remarks to the 1985 meeting of Salomon Brothers' managing directors as they celebrated the firm's 75th anniversary:

"The pace of change has continued to accelerate, and any summary that I might give would be most noteworthy for its omissions. Records are made to be broken and this seems to be what we are about. Tonight we can all look back on our 75 years of achievement and the contributions of the people of Salomon Brothers to the social and financial well-being of the communities, institutions and governments who are our clients. The principles that were set forth by Arthur Salomon 75 years ago are worth repeating, and I quote: 'I am certain that no person can succeed in Wall Street who is not a worker and who does not value his integrity above all things.'

"Once again, I look forward to the challenges and opportunities which will present themselves. I believe that this group of people in this room tonight and the 3,000-plus other Salomon people around the world will be challenged more than ever before. The opportunities, with our sense of commitment, are as great as they have ever been, and I in my imagination cannot even conceive of what shall be. I only know that my pride in having worked with all of you is great. I hope that the pleasures of this dedicated and fruitful life are enjoyed as much by you."

Footnotes

Chapter I

1. Mark Sullivan, *Our Times: The United States, 1900-1925* (New York: Scribner's, 1932), vol. 4, pp. 541-73 *passim*.
2. According to one who knew him, "He used to walk around Wall Street with a paper in his pocket — sell 50, sell 100 — and make a sixteenth on them or something like that." Morton and Ida Webster Interview, April 2, 1977.
3. William Salomon Interview, December 28, 1983.
4. Benjamin Levy Interview, March 9, 1977.
5. *The New York Times*, January 2, 1910.
6. Sereno Pratt, *The Work of Wall Street* (New York: Appleton, 1921), 3rd ed., pp. 37, 52-53, 132.
7. Benjamin Levy Interview, May 23, 1977.
8. C.A.E. Goodhart, *The New York Money Market and the Finance of Trade, 1900-1913* (Cambridge: Harvard University Press, 1969), p. 216.
9. Benjamin Levy Interviews, March 9; August 1, 1977.
10. Benjamin Levy Interview, March 9, 1977.
11. Daniel Kelly Interview, December 29, 1983.
12. Goodhart, *The New York Money Market*, p. 217.
13. Lawrence Chamberlain, *The Work of the Bond House* (New York: Moody's, 1912), pp. 49-50.
14. Stanley Jacobs Interview, April 18, 1977. Jacobs claims that Bernheim "put $150,000 into the firm."

Chapter II

1. 62nd United States Congress, 3rd session, *Hearings and Report of the Committee Appointed Pursuant to House Regulations 429 and 504 to Investigate the Concentration of Control of Money and Credit* (Washington, D.C.: USGPO, 1913), p. 150.
2. Alexander Dana Noyes, *Financial Chapters of the War* (New York: Scribner's, 1916); John Clark, *The Costs of the World War to the American People* (New Haven: Yale University Press, 1931).
3. Stanley Jacobs Interview, April 18, 1977.
4. Arthur K. Salomon, "New Phases on the Money Market — Business in Acceptances the Feature of an Interesting Year," *The New York Times*, January 2, 1916.

5. *The New York Times,* January 2, 1919; Vincent Carosso, *Investment Banking in America: A History* (Cambridge: Harvard University Press, 1970), p. 224.

6. Arthur K. Salomon, "Acceptance Now Has a Large Market," *New York Herald,* January 5, 1922.

7. Arthur K. Salomon, "A 'Forward Market' for Acceptances," *The Street,* June 4, 1921.

8. David Finkle Interview, March 10, 1977; "Don't play golf with Arthur. He'll start to swing and then he'll say, 'What did the 4¼s do?'" William Pollock Interview, April 19, 1977.

9. Abraham Eller Interview, May 18, 1977; David Finkle Interview, March 10, 1977.

10. Charles Simon Interview, August 9, 1977.

11. Abraham Eller Interview, May 18, 1977.

12. Harry Brown Interview, March 18, 1977.

13. Benjamin Levy Interview, March 9, 1977.

14. Harry Brown Interview, October 3, 1977.

15. William Morris Interview, April 18, 1977.

16. Jonas Ottens Interview, May 16, 1977; William Morris Interview, April 18, 1977.

17. Jonas Ottens Interview, May 16, 1977; Robert Quinn Interview, October 3, 1977; William Morris Interview, April 18, 1977.

18. Abraham Eller Interview, May 18, 1977.

19. Charles Simon Interview, September 15, 1977.

20. Jonas Ottens Interview, December 15, 1983.

21. Sidney Grobert Interview, June 28, 1984.

22. *New York Post,* December 15, 1924.

23. Eller believed that this act saved the company from bankruptcy during the 1929 market crash. Abraham Eller Interview, May 18, 1977.

24. A.R. Horr, *Embarrassing Dollars: And Hints to Their Holders.* (New York: Harper & Bros., 1935), p. 88.

Chapter III

1. David Finkle Interview, March 10, 1977; Jonas Ottens Interview, May 16, 1977.

2. Jane Bernheim Interview, December 14, 1983.

3. Morton and Ida Webster Interview, April 2, 1977.

4. "They wanted to get him out of the business. He wasn't contributing and he was getting a large percentage of the earnings." — David Finkle Interview, March 10, 1977; Stanley Jacobs Interview, April 18, 1977; Jonas Ottens Interview, May 16, 1977.

5. William Pollock Interview, April 19, 1977.

6. "Ben Levy's greatest attribute was, number one, his ability to remain calm — or seem to remain calm — under almost any condition. Number two, the fact that he knew every pin dropping. He knew every $500 bond trade. He knew everything that was going on in the shop . . . ." Harry Brown Interview, October 3, 1977.

7. When asked why Levy hadn't gone to Chicago, Eller responded, "Oh, no. They couldn't spare Ben away from his fulcrum." Abraham Eller Interview, May 18, 1977.

8. "I think Herbert Salomon frightened Abe Eller. The trouble with Abe Eller was that he was easily frightened." Harry Brown Interview, March 18, 1977.

9. Stanley Jacobs Interview, April 18, 1977.

10. Morton and Ida Webster Interview, April 2, 1977.

11. Chris Welles, *The Last Days of the Club* (New York: Dutton, 1975), p. 45.

12. Charles Abbott, *Financing Business During the Transition* (New York: McGraw-Hill, 1946), p. 19.

13. Jonas Ottens Interview, May 16, 1977.

14. Abraham Eller Interview, May 18, 1977; Daniel Kelly Interview, December 29, 1983.

15. Michael Parrish, *Securities Regulation and the New Deal* (New Haven: Yale University Press, 1970), pp. 187-88.

16. Joel Seligman, *The Transformation of Wall Street: A History of the Securities and Exchange Commission and Modern Corporate Finance* (Boston: Houghton Mifflin, 1982), pp. 111-14.

17. *Ibid.*, p. 115.

18. Morton and Ida Webster Interview, April 2, 1977; Conversation with Jonas Ottens, January 9, 1984.

19. *The New York Times*, March 27, 1935.

20. Arthur Schlesinger, Jr., *The Coming of the New Deal* (Boston: Houghton Mifflin, 1949), p. 468; *The New York Times*, January 3, 1937; Seligman, *The Transformation of Wall Street*, p. 116.

21. *A History of Morgan Stanley*, unpublished manuscript.

22. United States District Court, New York (Southern District), *Corrected Opinion of Harold R. Medina, United States Circuit Judge, in United States of America v. Henry S. Morgan, Harold Stanley, et al., doing business as Morgan Stanley & Co. et al.* (New York, 1954 ed.), pp. 58-63, 88-92.

23. Robert Sobel, *The Big Board: A History of the New York Stock Market* (New York: Free Press, 1965), p. 298.

24. Charles Simon Interview, August 9, 1977.

25. Robert Sobel, *The Great Bull Market: Wall Street in the 1920s* (New York: Norton, 1968), pp. 79-80.

26. Jonas Ottens Memo to Mel Adams, date unknown.

27. *The New York Times*, September 4-15, 1937; United States District Court, New York, *Corrected Opinion of Harold R. Medina*.

28. Sidney Homer Interview, April 20, 1981.

29. Jonas Ottens Interview, May 16, 1977; Sidney Homer Interview, April 20, 1981.

30. Randolph Paul, *Taxation in the United States* (Boston: Little, Brown, 1954), pp. 294-348.

31. Charles Simon Interview, September 15, 1977.

Chapter IV

1. Irving Kaufman Interview, January 26, 1984.

2. Charles Simon Interview, August 9, 1977.

3. Harry Brown Interview, March 18, 1977.

4. *Ibid.*

5. 87th United States Congress, 1st Session, Joint Economic Committee, *Variability of Private Investment in Plant and Equipment* (Washington, D.C.: USGPO, 1962), pp. 40-41.

6. Sidney Homer and Richard I. Johannesen, *The Price of Money, 1946 to 1969* (New Brunswick: Rutgers University Press, 1969), p. 3.

7. United States Bureau of the Census, *Historical Statistics of the United States, Colonial Times to 1970* (Washington, D.C.: USGPO, 1975), p. 1003.

8. Peter Drucker, *The Unseen Revolution: How Pension Fund Socialism Came to America* (New York: Harper & Row, 1976), pp. 7-8.

9. Robert Sobel, *Inside Wall Street: Continuity and Change in the Financial District* (New York: Norton, 1977), pp. 217-42.

10. Charles Simon Interview, January 31, 1984.

11. Robert Sobel, *NYSE: A History of the New York Stock Exchange, 1935-1975* (New York: Weybright & Talley, 1975), pp. 292-93.

12. Harry Brown Interview, March 18, 1977.

13. Morton and Ida Webster Interview, April 2, 1977.

14. Cary Reich, *Financier: The Biography of André Meyer* (New York: Morrow, 1983), p. 136; Gilbert Burck, "Man in a $100 Million Jam," *Fortune*, July, 1960, pp. 104-109; William Zeckendorf, *The Autobiography of William Zeckendorf* (New York: Holt, Rinehart & Winston, 1970), pp. 123-25.

15. Morton and Ida Webster Interview, April 2, 1977.

16. Most of the venture capital investments turned out badly; however, one of the good companies was Haloid Xerox. Had Salomon retained these shares, profits on them would have more than compensated for losses elsewhere. Daniel Kelly Interview, May 25, 1977.

17. Harry Brown Interview, October 3, 1977; *The New York Times*, January 27, 1956.

18. Jonas Ottens Interview, May 16, 1977; Harry Brown Interview, October 3, 1977.

19. Carol Loomis, "Living It Up in a 'Salomon-Sized' World," *Fortune*, April 1970, p. 127.

20. John Gutfreund, then a trader at the municipal desk, recalled Smutny arriving in the morning, scanning rail car shipments (to discover how Rail-Trailer was doing) and shouting, "How are the Smutnies?" referring to the Memphis bonds. John Gutfreund Interview, April 25, 1984.

21. Irving Kaufman Interview, January 26, 1984.

22. John Allan, "Wall Street Profile: A Successful Big-Time Trader," *The New York Times*, April 11, 1965.

23. William Salomon Interview, December 28, 1983; Harry Brown Interview, October 3, 1977.

24. Daniel Kelly Interview, December 29, 1983; Smutny became a partner at R.W. Pressprich & Co., and later went to Francis I. duPont. He died in 1974 at the age of 76. *The New York Times*, November 2, 1974.

25. Gedale Horowitz Interview, February 24, 1984.

Chapter V

1. John Brooks, *The Go-Go Years* (New York: Weybright & Talley, 1973), p. 264.

2. William Salomon Interview, February 10, 1984; John Gutfreund Interview, April 25, 1984; Gedale Horowitz Interview, February 24, 1984.

3. Sidney Grobert Interview, June 1, 1984.

4. Allan Fine Interview, June 24, 1984.

5. Vincent Murphy Interview, March 8, 1984.

6. *Barron's*, February 6, 1961.

7. Harry Brown Interview, March 18, 1984; John Gutfreund Interview, April 25, 1984.

8. Gedale Horowitz Interview, February 24, 1984.

9. Sidney Homer, *Fun With Bonds: An Autobiography of a Career*, unpublished ms. c 1977.

10. "Homer: Bard of the Bond Market," *Business Week*, September 23, 1967, p. 116.

11. Henry Kaufman Interview, July 18, 1984.

12. Fred Bleakley, "Henry Kaufman: Portrait of the Economist as an Activist," *Institutional Investor*, January 1972, pp. 49-50.

13. Henry Kaufman Interview, July 18, 1984; Irwin Ross, "How Henry Kaufman Gets It Right," *Fortune*, May 18, 1981, pp. 96, 98.

14. Daniel Kelly Interview, May 25, 1977; *The New York Times*, May 27, 1979.

15. The firms were: Morgan Stanley; Kuhn, Loeb; Smith Barney; Lehman Brothers; Glore Forgan; Kidder Peabody; Goldman, Sachs; White Weld; Eastman Dillon; Drexel; First Boston; Dillon, Read; Blyth; Harriman Ripley; Stone & Webster; Harris Hall; and Union Securities.

16. Carosso, *Investment Banking in America: A History*, pp. 493-94; *The New York Times*, September 23, 1953 and March 15, 1954.

17. *The New York Times*, October 23-26, 1962; William Salomon Interview, February 10, 1984.

18. Gedale Horowitz Interview, February 24, 1984.

19. *Ibid.*

20. John Gutfreund Interview, April 25, 1984; Jason Elsas Interview, July 3, 1984.

21. Jonas Ottens memo to Mel Adams, date unknown; John Gutfreund Interview, April 25, 1984.

22. Allan, "Wall Street Profile," *The New York Times*, April 11, 1965.

23. William Salomon Interview, February 10, 1984.

24. *Investment Dealers' Digest*, 1962-1964.

25. Allan, *loc. cit.*

Chapter VI

1. *New York Journal-American*, December 1, 1963.

2. Michael Jensen, *The Financiers: The World of the Great Wall Street Investment Banking Houses* (New York: Weybright & Talley, 1976), pp. 7-8; Robert Sobel, *The Worldly Economists* (New York: Free Press, 1980), pp. 221-30.

3. Gedale Horowitz Interview, February 24, 1984.

4. Vincent Murphy Interview, March 8, 1984.

5. John Gutfreund Interview, April 25, 1984.

6. "The Toughest Kid in Block Trading," *Business Week*, October 4, 1969, pp. 114-15.

7. Richard Rosenthal Interview, April 6, 1984.

8. *The Wall Street Journal*, May 30, 1962.

9. 88th United States Congress, 1st Session, *Report of the Special Study of the Securities Markets of the Securities and Exchange Commission* (Washington, D.C.: USGPO), Pt. 2, Ch. VI, pp. 110-21; Pt. 4, Ch. XIII, p. 859.

10. John Gutfreund Interview, April 25, 1984; Gedale Horowitz Interview, February 24, 1984.

11. Allan Pessin Lecture, June 8, 1983.

12. Stanley Shopkorn Lecture, October 11, 1983.

13. Beth McGoldrick, "Jay Perry's Biggest Trade," *Institutional Investor*, September, 1982, pp. 85-88.

14. "The Toughest Kid in Block Trading," *op. cit.*, p. 114; C. Welles, *The Last Days of the Club*, p. 46; Carol Loomis, "Living It Up in a 'Salomon-Sized' World," *Fortune*, April, 1970.

15. Vincent Murphy Interview, March 8, 1984.

16. *Ibid.*

17. Allan Fine Interview, June 24, 1984.

18. *Ibid.*

Chapter VII

1. In 1959 Robert Triffin warned that without the American balance of payments deficits, there would develop a dollar shortage which would strangle world trade, but if the deficits continued, foreigners would exchange surplus dollars for gold. This was known as the "Triffin Dilemma."

2. Michael Moffitt, *The World's Money: International Banking from Bretton Woods to the Brink of Insolvency* (New York: Simon & Schuster, 1983), pp. 35-40; M.S. Mendelsohn, *Money on the Move: The Modern International Capital Market* (New York: McGraw-Hill, 1980), pp. 3-16.

3. Edward Malca, *Pension Funds and Other Institutional Investors* (Lexington, Mass.: Lexington Books, 1975), pp. 107-8.

4. "Ira Harris: Chicago's Big Dealmaker," *Business Week*, June 25, 1979, p.72.

5. Jason Elsas Interview, July 3, 1984.

6. Steven Grand-Jean Lecture, August 24, 1982.

7. "A Maverick Pushes into Wall Street's Club," *Business Week*, April 3, 1978, p. 82

8. *Ibid.*, p. 77.

9. Terrence Connelly Lecture, September 19, 1983.

10. "Ira Harris: Chicago's Big Dealmaker," *loc. cit.*

11. Mendelsohn, *Money on the Move*, pp. 32-34; Gunter Dufey and Ian Giddy, *The International Money Market* (Englewood Cliffs, N.J.: Prentice-Hall, 1978), pp. 111-12

12. Anthony Sampson, *The Money Lenders: Bankers and a World in Turmoil* (New York: Viking, 1981), p. 110.

13. Moffitt, *The World's Money*, pp. 44-45

14. Richard Schmeelk Interview, March 18, 1984; John Gutfreund Interview, April 25, 1984.

15. Tessa Oxtoby Interview, February 12, 1984: Robert Scully Lecture, August 24, 1983.

16. Richard Schmeelk Interview, March 18, 1984; John Gutfreund Interview, April 25, 1984.

17. Mendelsohn, *Money on the Move*, pp. 95-97.

18. Moffitt, *The World's Money*, p. 60; Dufey and Giddy, *The International Money Market*, pp. 214-15; R.B. Johnson, *The Economics of the Euro-Market* (New York: St. Martin's Press, 1982), p. 26.

19. Moffitt, *The World's Money*, p. 184; Sampson, *The Money Lenders*, pp. 129-39; Johnson, *The Economics of the Euro-Market*, pp. 29-30.

20. Robert Scully Lecture, August 24, 1983.

21. Peter Clarke Lecture, January 15, 1983.

22. George Hutchinson Interview, June 1, 1984.

23. Cary Reich, "Salomon: The Spectacular Debut of an International Upstart," *Institutional Investor*, January, 1978, p. 20.

24. *Ibid.*, p. 30.

Chapter VIII

1. Sobel, *Inside Wall Street*, pp. 54-56, 67-90; Sobel, *NYSE*, pp. 346-48; Welles, *The Last Days of the Club*, pp. 52-60.

2. *Institutional Investor*, April, 1971, p. 32.

3. Welles, *The Last Days of the Club*, p. 106; Sobel, *NYSE*, p. 350.

4. *Ibid.*, p. 330.

5. Sobel, *The Last Bull Market*, pp. 214-15.

6. Stanley Shopkorn Lecture, October 11, 1983; Allan Pessin Lecture, June 8, 1983; Salomon Brothers, *Annual Review, 1972*, p. 3.

7. Stanley Shopkorn Lecture, October 11, 1983; Edwin Olsen Lecture, June 10, 1983.

8. John Gutfreund Interview, April 25, 1984.

9. Salomon Brothers, *Annual Review, 1973*, p. 2.

10. Charles Morris, *The Cost of Good Intentions: New York City and the Liberal Experiment, 1960-1975* (New York: Norton, 1980), pp. 220-30.

11. Sobel, *The Worldly Economists*, p. 229.

12. *The Wall Street Journal* and *The New York Times*, June 17-July 4, 1975.

13. John O'Brien Interview, May 24, 1984.

14. Michael Frinquelli Interview, May 18, 1984; "GEICO Builds on New Confidence," *The New York Times*, August 16, 1979; Beth Brophy, "After the Fall, and Rise," *Forbes*, February 2, 1981.

15. "An Interview with John Gutfreund," *Euromoney*, October, 1979.

16. "A Maverick Pushes into Wall Street's Club," *Business Week*, April 3, 1978, p. 85.

17. John Gutfreund Lecture, June 18, 1983.

Chapter IX

1. Cary Reich, "Salomon: The Spectacular Debut of an International Upstart," *Institutional Investor*, January 1978, p. 23.

2. Marcia Stigums, *The Money Market* (Homewood, Ill.: Dow Jones-Irwin, 1983), pp. 216-17, 220.

3. Dana Thomas, "Ginnie Mae's Kid Sister," *Barron's*, November 14, 1977, p. 3.

4. Robert Dall, "The Merging of the Mortgage and Capital Markets," Speech, January 1981.

5. Robert Dall Interview, May 24, 1984.

6. Linda Sandler, "The Mortgage-Backed Securities Bonanza," *Institutional Investor*, March 1984, pp. 84-85.

7. Lewis Ranieri Interview, May 18, 1984.

8. Lewis Ranieri Lecture, June 5, 1982.

9. "The Whiz Kid of Wall Street's Home-Mortgage Boom," *Business Week*, June 11, 1984, pp. 140-41.

10. Lewis Ranieri Interview, May 18, 1984.

11. "The Mortgaged-Backed Securities Bonanza," *loc. cit.*; Robert Dall, "Meeting Single-Family Mortgage Demand During the 1980s," Speech, March 17, 1982.

12. Martin Mayer, *The Money Bazaar: Understanding the Banking Revolution Around Us* (New York: Dutton, 1984), pp. 3-4.

13. "Now Salomon Is the Marrying Kind," *The Economist*, August 8, 1981, p. 63.

14. J. Steven Manolis Lecture, February 8, 1983.

15. David LaGesse, "Mortgage Loan Traders Being Lured with Big Bucks," *American Banker*, March 23, 1984, p. 9.

16. Tim Carrington, "The Day Can Be Tense at Salomon Brothers," *The Wall Street Journal*; Tim Carrington, "Salomon Plans to Pay Generous Bonuses to Retain Employees after Phibro Merger," *The Wall Street Journal*, August 7, 1981.

17. Thomas Strauss Interview, July 3, 1984.

18. Gedale Horowitz Lecture, August 10, 1983; "A Wall Street Leader at Grips with Deregulation," *Euromoney*, September 1982, p. 283.

19. *The Wall Street Journal*, June 3, 15, August 31, 1981.

20. *Ibid.*, May 12, 1981.

21. "A Trading Superpower Is Born," *Business Week*, August 17, 1981, p. 24.

22. Reich, *Financier: The Biography of André Meyer*, pp. 66-68; Chris Welles, "The Colossus of Phibro," *Institutional Investor*, December 1981, p. 40.

23. *The New York Times*, May 23, 1984.

24. William Vouté Interview, July 11, 1984.

25. "A Wall Street Leader at Grips with Deregulation," *op. cit.*, p. 285; "Now Salomon Is the Marrying Kind," *op. cit.*, pp. 63-64.

26. "Salomon Plans to Pay Generous Bonuses," *loc. cit.*

27. John Gutfreund Interview, April 25, 1984.

28. "A Trading Superpower Is Born," *op cit.*, p. 25; "The Colossus of Phibro," *op. cit.*, pp. 40, 53.

29. "A Wall Street Leader at Grips with Deregulation," *op. cit.*, p. 283.

Chapter X

1. "How to Shed Debt and Add Equity," *Business Week*, October 19, 1981, p. 120.

2. "The Newest Way to Wipe Out Old Debt," *Business Week*, August 9, 1982, pp. 65-66.

3. Beth McGoldrick, "The Great Debate About Debt-Equity Swaps," *Institutional Investor*, October 1982, pp. 197-204.

4. Salomon Brothers, *Annual Review, 1983*, p. 33.

5. "The Whiz Kid of Wall Street's Home-Mortgage Boom," *op. cit.*, p. 141.

6. Neil Osborn, "The Furor Over Shelf Registration," *Institutional Investor*, June 1982, pp. 61-71.

7. "A Wall Street Leader at Grips with Deregulation," *op. cit.*, p. 280.

8. *Annual Review, 1983*, p. 11.

9. Michael Moritz and Barrett Seaman, *Going for Broke: The Chrysler Story* (New York: Doubleday, 1981), pp. 215-16.

10. *Ibid.*, p. 335.

11. Edward Scharff, "The Clincher for Chrysler," *Institutional Investor*, July 1983, p. 224.

12. *Annual Review, 1983,* pp. 25-26.

13. Carol Loomis, "The Morning After at Phibro-Salomon," *Fortune*, January 10, 1983, pp. 74, 79.

14. *Ibid.*

15. *The New York Times*, May 23, 1984.

16. *The Wall Street Journal*, June 1, 1984.

17. *The Wall Street Journal*, August 7; October 5, 1984.

Chapter XI

1. All quotations from Salomon Brothers personnel in this section derive from interviews and training session lectures, 1981-84.

About the Author

Robert Sobel, a professor of business history at New College of Hofstra University in Hempstead, New York, has been exploring and studying the financial district for over 30 years. A financial newspaper columnist for *Newsday*, he has written articles and reviews for *Barron's*, *The New York Times*, *The Wall Street Journal* and *Institutional Investor*. Mr. Sobel received his Ph.D. in history and economics from New York University, and is the author of the following books:

The Origins of Interventionism
The Big Board: A History of the New York Stock Market
The Great Bull Market: Wall Street in the 1920s
Panic on Wall Street
The Curbstone Brokers: The Origins of the American Stock
    Exchange
Conquest and Conscience: The United States in the 1840s
The Age of Giant Corporations
Amex: A History of the American Stock Exchange
Machines and Morality: The United States in the 1850s
Money Manias: Eras of Great Speculation in American History
For Want of a Nail . . . .: If Burgoyne Had Won at Saratoga
The Entrepreneurs
Herbert Hoover at the Onset of the Great Depression
N.Y.S.E.: A History of the New York Stock Exchange
The Manipulators: America in the Media Age
Inside Wall Street: Continuity and Change in the Financial
    District
The Fallen Colossus: The Great Crash of the Penn Central
They Satisfy: The Cigarette in American Life
The Last Bull Market: Wall Street in the 1960s
The Worldly Economists
IBM: Colossus in Transition
ITT: The Management of Opportunity
The Rise and Fall of the Conglomerate Kings
Car Wars
IBM vs. Japan: The Struggle for the Future

Bibliographical Note

Salomon Brothers was on the periphery of the Wall Street scene during much of the past three-quarters of a century. There was no mention of the firm in news stories in either *The New York Times* or *The Wall Street Journal* from its founding in 1910 until the mid-1930s, and precious little for the next twenty years. Then, from the late 1950s to the present, articles about Salomon Brothers appeared with increasing regularity not only in the daily press, but in the more important business magazines as well.

Necessarily, my most important sources for the initial two-thirds of the story have been the recollections of Salomon Brothers partners, employees, and others in the financial world of the time, many of whom were interviewed and without whose cooperation this book could not have been written. In addition, I have called upon my earlier experiences in the financial district in an attempt to recreate the atmosphere of the times, the milieu in which Salomon Brothers functioned.

Interviews, together with video tapes of Salomon Brothers training sessions, were prime sources for the rest of the history, though fortunately they were augmented by reports in the daily and weekly press.

Sources have been credited in the footnotes to this work. A list of the more important books and periodicals follows, along with a list of those who were interviewed in the research phase.

To all who assisted in my endeavors, heartfelt thanks, especially to Mel Adams, Craig Lewis, Charles Brophy, Anne Cordasco, Ronne Mandelker and Allison Chisolm of Adams & Rinehart, and to Ed Rowe of Stead Young & Rowe, all of whose generous cooperation is most appreciated. I would also like to thank Bill Tierney of Salomon Brothers, whose interest in the firm's history and willingness to assist one who groped after truth was exceptional. Finally, David Harrop edited the book with his customary skill, intelligence, and good humor, while Ilene Cherna scoured galleries and private collections for the pictures.

Books

Abbott, Charles. *Financing Business During the Transition.* New York: McGraw-Hill, 1946.

———. *The New York Bond Market, 1920–1930.* Cambridge: Harvard University Press, 1937.

Brooks, John. *The Go-Go Years.* New York: Weybright & Talley, 1973.

Carosso, Vincent. *Investment Banking in America: A History.* Cambridge: Harvard University Press, 1970.

Chamberlain, Lawrence. *The Work of the Bond House.* New York: Moody's, 1912.

Clark, John. *The Costs of the World War to the American People.* New Haven: Yale University Press, 1931.

Drucker, Peter. *The Unseen Revolution: How Pension Fund Socialism Came to America.* New York: Harper & Row., 1976.

Dufey, Gunter, and Ian Giddy. *The International Money Market.* Englewood Cliffs, N.J.: Prentice-Hall, 1978.

Friend, Irwin, James Longstreet, Morris Mendelson, Ervin Miller, and Arleigh Hess, Jr. *Investment Banking and the New Issues Market.* Philadelphia: University of Pennsylvania, 1965.

Goldsmith, Raymond, ed. *Institutional Investors and Corporate Stock — A Background Study.* New York: National Bureau of Economic Research, 1973.

Goodhart, C.A.E. *The New York Money Market and the Finance of Trade, 1900–1913.* Cambridge: Harvard University Press, 1969.

Greef, Albert. *The Commercial Paper House in the United States.* Cambridge: Harvard University Press, 1938.

Griffiss, Bartow. *The New York Call Money Market.* New York: Ronald, 1925.

Haney, Lewis, Lyman Logan, and Henry Gavens. *Brokers' Loans.* New York: Harper & Bros., 1932.

Holbrook, Stewart. *The Age of the Moguls.* New York: Doubleday, 1953.

Homer, Sidney. *A History of Interest Rates: 2000 B.C. to the Present.* New Brunswick: Rutgers University Press, 1963.

———. *An Analytical Record of Yields and Yield Spreads.* New York: Salomon Brothers, 1962.

Homer, Sidney, and Richard I.Johannesen. *The Price of Money, 1946 to 1969*. New Brunswick: Rutgers University Press, 1969.

Horr, A.R. *Embarrassing Dollars: And Hints to Their Holders*. New York: Harper & Bros., 1935.

Irwin, Robert. *The New Mortgage Game*. New York: McGraw-Hill, 1982.

Jensen, Michael. *The Financiers: The World of the Great Wall Street Investment Banking Houses*. New York: Weybright & Talley, 1976.

Johnson, R.B. *The Economics of the Euro-Market: History, Theory and Policy*. New York: St. Martin's Press, 1982.

Kennan, George. *E.H. Harriman: A Biography*. Boston: Houghton Mifflin, 1922.

Kidd, Phillip. *Mortgage Banking 1963 to 1972: A Financial Intermediary in Transition*. West Lafayette, Ind.: Purdue Research Foundation, 1977.

King, Kenneth. *U.S. Monetary Policy and European Responses in the 1980s*. London: Routledge & Kegan Paul, 1982.

LeBaron, Dean. *Ins and Outs of Institutional Investing*. Chicago: Nelson Hall, 1976.

Letters from Prominent Financiers on Interest Rates Written in the Year 1899. New York: Scudder, Stevens & Clark, 1899.

Malca, Edward. *Pension Funds and Other Institutional Investors*. Lexington, Mass.: Lexington Books, 1975.

Manne, Henry, and Ezra Solomon, eds. *Wall Street in Transition: The Emerging System and Its Impact on the Economy*. New York: New York University Press, 1974.

Mayer, Martin. *The Bankers*. New York: Weybright & Talley, 1974.

———. *The Money Bazaar: Understanding the Banking Revolution Around Us*. New York: Dutton, 1984.

Mendelsohn, M.S. *Money on the Move: The Modern International Capital Market*. New York: McGraw-Hill, 1980.

Moffitt, Michael. *The World's Money: International Banking from Bretton Woods to the Brink of Insolvency*. New York: Simon & Schuster, 1983.

Moritz, Michael, and Barrett Seaman. *Going for Broke: The Chrysler Story*. New York: Doubleday, 1981.

Morris, Charles. *The Cost of Good Intentions: New York City and the Liberal Experiment, 1960-1975*. New York: Norton, 1980.

Muer, Ross, and Carl White. *Over The Long Term . . . The Story of J. & W. Seligman & Co*. New York: J. & W. Seligman, 1964.

Noyes, Alexander Dana. *Financial Chapters of the War*. New York: Scribner's, 1916.

―――. *Forty Years of American Finance*. New York: Putnam's, 1909.

Parrish, Michael. *Securities Regulation and the New Deal*. New Haven: Yale University Press, 1970.

Paul, Randolph. *Taxation in the United States*. Boston: Little, Brown, 1954.

Pierce, Phyllis. *The Dow Jones Averages, 1885-1980*. Homewood, Ill.: Dow Jones-Irwin, 1983.

Pratt, Sereno. *The Work of Wall Street*. New York: Appleton, 1921.

Reich, Cary. *Financier: The Biography of André Meyer*. New York: Morrow, 1983.

Rice, Samuel, ed. *Fundamentals of Investment*. Chicago: Shaw, 1926.

Sakolski, A.M. *Principles of Investment*. New York: Ronald, 1925.

Sampson, Anthony. *The Money Lenders: Bankers and a World in Turmoil*. New York: Viking, 1981.

Schlesinger, Arthur, Jr. *The Coming of the New Deal*. Boston: Houghton Mifflin, 1949.

Schultz, William, and M.R. Caine. *Financial Development of the United States*. New York: Prentice-Hall, 1937.

Seidler, Lee, Frederick Andrews, and Marc Epstein. *The Equity Funding Papers: The Anatomy of a Fraud*. Santa Barbara, Cal.: Wiley, 1977.

Seligman, Joel. *The Transformation of Wall Street: A History of the Securities and Exchange Commission and Modern Corporate Finance*. Boston: Houghton Mifflin, 1982.

Sobel, Robert. *The Big Board: A History of the New York Stock Market*. New York: Free Press, 1965.

―――. *The Great Bull Market: Wall Street in the 1920s*. New York: Norton, 1968.

―――. *Inside Wall Street: Continuity and Change in the Financial District*. New York: Norton, 1977.

―――. *The Worldly Economists*. New York: Free Press, 1980.

Soble, Ronald, and Robert Dallos. *The Impossible Dream: The Equity Funding Story, The Fraud of the Century*. New York: Putnam's, 1975.

Soldofsky, Robert. *Institutional Holdings of Common Stocks, 1900-2000*. Ann Arbor: University of Michigan, 1971.

Stigums, Marcia. *The Money Market*. Homewood, Ill.: Dow Jones-Irwin, 1983.

Sullivan, Mark. *Our Times: The United States, 1900–1925.* Vol. 4: *The War Begins, 1909-1914.* New York: Scribner's, 1932.

United States Bureau of the Census. *Historical Statistics of the United States, Colonial Times to 1970.* Washington, D.C.: USGPO, 1975.

United States District Court, New York (Southern District). *Corrected Opinion of Harold R. Medina, United States Circuit Judge, in United States of America v. Henry S. Morgan, Harold Stanley, et al., doing business as Morgan Stanley & Co. et al.* New York: 1954 ed.

Welles, Chris. *The Last Days of the Club.* New York: Dutton, 1975.

Wheeler, George. *J.P. Morgan and Friends: The Anatomy of a Myth.* Englewood Cliffs, N.J.: Prentice-Hall, 1973.

Willis, H. Parker, and Jules Bogen. *Investment Banking.* New York: Harper & Bros., 1936.

Zeckendorf, William. *The Autobiography of William Zeckendorf.* New York: Holt, Rinehart & Winston, 1970.

Periodicals and Newspapers

American Banker
Barron's
Business Week
The Economist
Euromoney
Forbes
Fortune

Institutional Investor
New York Post
The New York Times
Newsweek
Time
Wall Street Letter
The Wall Street Journal

Interviews

Bernheim, Jane. *December 14, 1983.*
Brown, Harry. *March 18; October 3, 1977.*
Coats, Craig. *June 20, 1984.*
Dall, Robert. *May 24, 1984.*
DeLucia, David. *February 14, 1984.*
Dubrow, Neil. *June 20, 1984.*
Eller, Abraham. *May 18, 1977.*
Elsas, Jason. *July 3, 1984.*
Fine, Allan. *June 24, 1984.*
Finkle, David. *March 10, 1977.*
Frinquelli, Michael. *May 18, 1984.*
Gould, Charles. *June 17, 1984.*
Grand-Jean, Richard. *November 26, 1984.*
Grobert, Sidney. *June 1; June 28, 1984.*
Gutfreund, John. *April 25, 1984.*
Homer, Sidney. *April 20, 1981.*
Horowitz, Gedale. *February 24, 1984.*
Hutchinson, George. *June 1, 1984.*
Jacobs, Stanley. *April 18, 1977.*
Kaufman, Henry. *July 18, 1984.*

Kaufman, Irving. *January 26, 1984.*
Kelly, Daniel. *May 25, 1977; December 29, 1983.*
Kronthal, Jeffrey. *June 1, 1984.*
Lechtman, Ira. *October 13, 1977.*
Levy, Benjamin. *March 9; May 23; August 1, 1977.*
McVeigh, Charles. *February 13, 1984.*
Massey, James. *July 11, 1984.*
Morris, William. *April 18, 1977.*
Murphy, Vincent. *March 8, 1984.*
O'Brien, John. *May 24, 1984.*
Ottens, Jonas. *May 16, 1977; December 15, 1983.*
Oxtoby, Tessa. *February 12, 1984.*
Pollock, William. *April 19, 1977.*
Quinn, Robert. *October 3, 1977.*
Ranieri, Lewis. *May 18, 1984.*
Rosenthal, Richard. *April 6, 1984.*
Salomon, William. *December 28, 1983; February 10, 1984.*
Schmeelk, Richard. *March 18, 1984.*
Simon, Charles. *August 9; September 15, 1977; January 31, 1984.*
Strauss, Thomas. *July 3, 1984.*
Tierney, William. *June 27, 1984.*
Vouté, William. *July 11, 1984.*
Webster, Morton and Ida. *April 2, 1977.*

Index

Franklin National Bank, 132
Freeman, Merrill, 98, 100
Frinquelli, Michael, 150
Friswold, Frederick, 184
Funston, Keith, 66
futures market, 19–20

Gaertner, Clement, 32, 79, 81, 82, 98
Gaynor, William S., 1
General Motors Corp., 64, 186, 188
Getty Oil Co., 186
Getty, J. Paul, Trust, 186
Glass-Owen Act (1913), 15
Glass-Steagall Act of 1933, 51–52, 53
gold, 11, 118
Goldman, Sachs & Co., 55, 94, 101, 141, 168, 173, 188, 197;
    block trading, 108, 110, 142;
    corporate clients, 125
government bonds, viii, 5, 17–18, 24, 45, 54, 56, 58, 63
Government Employees Insurance Company (GEICO), x, 149–51
Government National Mortgage Association ("Ginnie Mae"), 159–63
Grand-Jean, Richard, 130, 133
Grand-Jean, Steven, 123
Graybar Building, 69
Great Bull Market, 34, 103, 111
Great Crash, 39, 40, 43
Great Depression, 20, 56, 57, 58
Grieder, Franklin, 82
Grobert, Sidney, 79
Guaranty Trust Company of New York, viii, 52
"Guerrilla Groups" (SB), ix, 100
Gulf Oil Co., 186
Gutfreund, John, xi, xii, 83–84, 92–93, 94–95, 107, 109, 121, 122, 123, 144,
    184, 199;
    became SB partner, 98;
    and GEICO rescue, 150–51;
    and SB International, 130, 137;
    management of SB, 152–58, 163, 165, 168, 170, 171, 178, 182, 193,
    194–95;
    management of SB during Chrysler rescue, 186–87;
    management of SB during Phibro merger, 173, 174, 175, 176, 177, 190,
    191–92;
    on SB, 201

International Business Machines Corp. (IBM), 124
international commercial paper, 18–19, 44
international finance, 125–28, 130–33, 153, 155
International Harvester Co., 186
International Paper Co., 124
investment banking, 51–52, 55, 90, 173;
    overseas opportunities, 132–33;
    SB and, x, 13, 86, 95, 111, 121–23, 125, 130, 133, 153, 178;
    see also mergers and acquisitions
Investors Mutual Inc., 66
Investors Planning Corp., 107

Jacobs, Stanley, 33
Japanese market, 134–36
Jarecki, Henry, 176
Jesselson, Ludwig, 171–72, 173, 189
Johnson, Lyndon, 115, 126
Johnson, William, 124
Jones, A. N., 52
Joseph, Stephen, 169

Kaufman, Henry, 87–89, 98, 102, 123, 153, 176, 194, 199;
    Comments on Credit (weekly commentary), 88;
    management of SB, 174, 178;
    on SB, 195–97
Kaufman, Irving, 32
Kearney, Daniel, 163
Keene, James, 103
Kelly, Daniel, 32, 33
Kelly, Donald, 122, 125
Kennedy, John, 142
Kennedy, Joseph, 46–47, 48
Kennedy administration, 126
"Kennedy Crash, The," 106
Knickerbocker Trust, 2
Korean War, 58
Kuhn, Loeb, 17, 52, 55, 168
Kuwait, 130